dangerous PRAYER

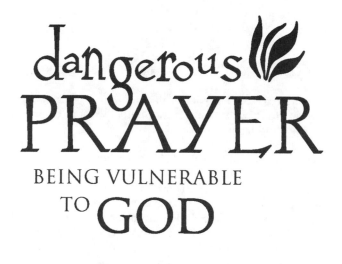

dangerous PRAYER

BEING VULNERABLE
TO GOD

William J. O'Malley, S.J.

LIGUORI
PUBLICATIONS

One Liguori Drive
Liguori, MO 63047-9999
(314) 464-2500

THIS BOOK IS FOR
WILLIAM PETER BLATTY
THEN, AND NOW.

TABLE
OF CONTENTS

PREFACE

It takes a dose of chutzpa to differ with so eminent a mind as Thomas Aquinas, but I have never been short on chutzpa. Aquinas and other medieval and Renaissance philosophers defined human beings as *animalia rationalia*: rational animals. But that classification smacks of rank reductionism; it leaves out too much that is essential in human beings, just as rank pessimism leaves out beer, babies, and books, and rank optimism ignores blizzards, landslides, and hangnails.

"Rational animal" reduces us to little more than apes with onboard computers. It ignores uniquely human activities that no ape or computer—or combination thereof—could dream of: imagination, understanding, wisdom, honor, ambition, self-sacrificing love. And it surely disregards prayer, which is a very real contact beyond space and time. All of these are properties not of the body or of the mind but of the human soul.

A newborn child, for the first year or so, looks like nothing more than a healthy little animal: eating, sleeping, watching, pooping—in general, just "doin' what comes natcherly." But unlike even the cleverest animal, the infant has the *potential* to be far, far more than merely "a sound mind in a sound

x

body." This yet-to-be-fully-formed infant has the chance to evolve—and continue to evolve—further and further along the human spectrum that stretches all the way from scarcely human beings like pushers and terrorists to Dorothy Day and Maxmilian Kolbe.

Unlike the highest-level animal, humans have an *invitation* to activate that potential: the human soul. But like all invitations, it can be refused—and, one fears, too often it is. You have only to look the length of a car on a commuter train to read all the frustration, world-weariness, and sadness in the dead-ended eyes pinched between the earpieces of portable tape players.

This book is merely a reiteration of an invitation written on the very fibers of your human soul and in the life, death, and resurrection of the Son of God—an invitation to the dangerous choice of praying intently and intensely.

How does one risk activating and energizing the human soul? Well, first you have to acknowledge—truly own—the fact that you do *have* a soul, a power to lift yourself out of the routine into the sublime. Until you do, you'll still be plodding along. Then you have to acknowledge that your soul is in fact a potential that needn't be activated; that you have to put forth the same effort to actualize your human spirit as you do to activate the potential of your body and mind.

Many people get "forced" into praying—"Did you say your prayers before you went to sleep last night?"—so that praying becomes merely something you have to do, either to placate a lonely and some-

times vindictive God or to wheedle a few favors out
of the Three of Them. Even in seminaries and con-
vents (at least until recently), men and women preparing to become professional pray-ers were merely
told, "We meditate for forty-five minutes at seven
a.m., and for thirty minutes at five p.m." And I don't
recall anyone around my time asking the perfectly
obvious and forgivable question: "Excuse me, please,
but…uh…how?"

That's what this book is all about.

To my (quite fallible but restless) mind, the teaching Church has always been working backwards: trying to make us Catholics before we've comprehended
the core of the Christian gospel; trying to make us
Christians before we've ever reasoned our way to the
existence of a loving Creator or wrestled with the
reality of death; and trying to make us theists before
we've ever become sensitive to the wonders of creation.

Since grace builds on nature (or not at all), you
have first to actualize a this-world sense of the
numinous: the sense aroused in us when we see a
snow-capped mountain at dawn, when we feel the
miracle of a baby's skin, when our hearts beat in
tempo with the *Hallelujah Chorus*. We feel the surge
of the sacred. Even without knowing God, the awe
we feel is an act of praise to the Great Surpriser who
dreamed up the trilobite and the giraffe and the hairy-
nosed wombat in defiance of reason and efficiency.

Then, when the spark of the soul has been ignited,
it can be led to try to make sense of it all: the beauty

and the filth, the nobility of some human souls and the degradation of others, the miracle of life and the puzzlement of death.

It is an urge to go beyond the dumb-animal acceptance of the status quo and to ask why things aren't as they "should be." Until one is curious about the meaning of human life, trying to find a personal philosophy that makes some coherence out of the chaos and a personally validated conscience that guides one's choices, the gospel doesn't have a chance. One has to go from *"They* tell me...." to "This *I* believe."

Only then is one ready to face that God-sized hunger Augustine knew when he said, "Our hearts are restless till they rest in Thee." Nature and art can be marvelously fulfilling. Study and learning can exhilarate the human spirit. Like every response to the numinous in nature and art, every hour of study is a prayer to the Truth who underlies it all. But there is still more. One craves union with the energizing Spirit beneath it all. And it is not enough simply to know *about* God. One wants to know *God.*

There, then, are the motivations behind this book: first, to invite you (or more precisely, to remind you that you have been invited all along) to activate your highest human potential, and then to remind you of the invitation of Jesus to risk coming even further into the heart of the Trinity family.

Twenty years ago, I wrote the core of this book. Now and again, people would see the title on my *curriculum vitae* and ask where they could get a copy. My only reply was "a secondhand bookshop or a seminary fire sale."

Recently, I dug this book out and read it again and, with uncharacteristic hubris, said, "Not bad," but not good enough either. In twenty years, even I could hardly help having learned a bit about people and about praying. So I tinkered, cut, reinforced, and here it is—a bit like Lazarus.

Some years ago a teacher of yoga read the original book and wrote to tell me he used it in his seminars. At the end of his letter, instead of the usual complimentary close such as "Very truly yours" or "Sincerely," he wrote: "I bow to the divine in you."

And even though we have never met, I bow to the divine in you. And I invite you to do the same.

William J. O'Malley, S.J.

INTRODUCTION

This is a very dangerous book. At least I hope it will be dangerous, in the same way that the gospels are surely dangerous. This book asks the reader to entertain the possibility that his or her life can be lived more intensely, though the price may be a lot of comfortable habits and attitudes. Even further, it asks that the reader experimentally surrender, for a quarter of an hour a day, dependence on the rational—the discursive intelligence—that balances budgets, works through projects, meets deadlines, figures things out. Instead, it asks you—the reader—to open up powers of the spirit within that you never suspected and allow the Spirit of God to take over. This book invites you to prayer—perhaps in new ways that are challenging, risky, and even dangerous.

Christian Doctrine v. Christian Experience

In that part of my life where I wore my "theater" hat (as opposed to my "teaching" hat), I wrote a musical called *Tender Is the Knight*. With mixed success, it was intended to be a satire on formal schooling, war, and other stupidities beloved of humankind. At the Knight School, all the young men drilled and drilled every day to slaughter dragons—though none of them had ever seen one. But there were always rumors. Meanwhile, up in the hills, young dragons snorted away trying to breathe fire and belch smoke in order to incinerate all those pink little knights—if they ever met one. Each side had heard such tales of the other. Of course, when a runaway young knight and a renegade young dragon meet one evening in the forest, they terrify each other half to death. But when they begin to talk as persons, when the things they've heard *about* each other give way to what they actually *experience* of each other, they become friends.

This musical showed the power of reality over rumor and demonstrated that personal contact can overthrow at least some of the mixed-up notions that cause trouble and tragedy. In much the same way, we need to "overthrow" our high falutin' notions of God and get to know Our Lord on a one-to-one basis. This is where prayer comes in; this is where arm's-length misinformation goes out.

When I was young, a great deal of religious education was just like the curriculum in the Knight School: the arming of reluctant young minds with ammunition to refute the perfidious and heretical arguments of those Protestants and Jews and Masons. There were whole armies of them, plotting to lure us from our side to their side. And all this despite the fact that many of our friends and neighbors and even relatives were members of these reputedly subversive groups. Still, at the time, that seemed the sole reason for religious education. Certainly, learning about prayer was not a high priority in this dragon-hunting phase of teaching youngsters about being Catholic.

Gradually, the churches saw how dumb the situation was and very wisely made peace. However, a great many Catholics had defined themselves solely as being "not Protestant": once that is taken away, what are we? And it is that loss of identity (which had been based on something so negative) that still makes some Catholics nervous today. "With all this disrespect for the Pope, with all these free-thinking theologians, without Latin, we're just like the Protestants!"

With the focus shifting away from knights versus dragons, a more practical problem then becomes: What *do* we teach our kids? The answers to that question have gone, I think, in two laudable but incomplete directions. One group uses banners, balloons, and lots of love words; groups like these show films about human problems and have endless discussions of human values. All well and good, but so do pagans. The other approach—or the other half of the same religion teacher—exposes Christian doctrine: explanations of the Creed, the sacraments, the constitution and history of the Church, and (gasp!) year-long moral debates. All good and academic, but much of it would gladden the heart of the most fastidious Pharisee.

We've gone for the heart; we've gone for the head. But somewhere along the line we lost what bonds the heart and the head together: the spirit, the soul, the self. We forgot that whole list of doctrines in the Creed begins with "*I* believe."

We've got impeccable human values; we've got organized Church rules. The one thing we've lost in the shuffle, though, is God—and the very real work it takes to maintain our relationship with him.

We have become so preoccupied with explaining the signposts which point to God—the sacraments, the rules, the structures, even Scripture, the Church, and the Mass—that we forgot to look in the direction they were all pointing. To a great extent, the God-signs became God-substitutes. We forgot to remember the Person who is the reason for all this fuss and, worse, we forgot to remember the reason God wanted all the fuss in the first place.

I trust God knew what they were doing on Mount Sinai, but it's too bad they had Moses come down with those two tablets of laws. People were so short-sighted—or so practical or so wedded to the tangible and numbing numbers—that they focused all their attention on the stone lists and forgot the light blazing from Moses' face, fresh from meeting God.

Jesus told us his purpose: "I have come to cast fire on the earth!" But as I look around at the Christian churches, I see lots of explanations and lots of debates, but precious little fire. Jesus also said: "I have come that they may have life, and have it abundantly!" (John 10:10). But as I look at my fellow Christians, I don't seem to see much more aliveness or love or freedom than I see in my friends who are Jews or pagans or even atheists.

There are even nominal Christians who tell me that what they (mistakenly) think being a Christian means ("all those rules and doctrines") is a positive hindrance to aliveness and love and freedom. If that's what they think being Christian means, I don't blame them.

This calcification of aliveness into rule-keeping is not restricted to the churches. Education sets out to be an exciting attempt to enliven minds but ends up very pleased with keeping good order. Businesses begin with a noble attempt to offer a quality product that will last but end up perfectly happy with making money. As John Gardner says, "The first sign of a dying society is when they issue a new edition of the rules."

Why does this happen? Perhaps because rules are easier to handle than love. Perhaps because doctrine is easier to teach than prayer. Perhaps because we are so conditioned to demand clear and distinct Cartesian ideas in classrooms, even in religious classrooms, that we shy away from introducing Christians to the very Persons who make all the signs that, while communicating their presence, are nonetheless inadequate to capture them.

This book, inadequate itself, proposes to set up that meeting between the essence and the signs, between the rules and the experience, between the rumor and the reality. This book attempts to teach prayer as a bridge between the heart and the head. In so doing, I hope finally to do that for which I was baptized and ordained: to help my brothers and sisters come truly alive.

The Discursive Mind v. the Receptive Spirit

6

Discursive intelligence analyzes, appraises, objectively judges. Most of our education tries to strengthen it; people who can analyze well not only get good jobs but are far better able to cope with the problems of life. I surely don't mean to denigrate it; on the contrary, half my time teaching is spent shouting, "Many people would rather die than think; and most of them do!"

Discursive intelligence also has a place in the teaching of theology and Christian doctrine. The unfortunate thing is that, in my experience, it has taken over and dominates almost all of what is called religious education. Knowing *about* God has replaced *knowing* God.

For the most part, we don't know persons analytically. And yet God—who, we are told even in the most analytic of theology classes, is a Person (three, in fact)—is treated as little more than a character in a novel or a figure in history. If we're to know God in any way other than the strictly and coldly academic mode, we have to approach God as we would approach any other person we want to know: person-to-person.

But we are great talkers and rather poor listeners. Even in prayer, we want to dominate, to tell God something he doesn't know, to change God's mind, and then be sure that the conversation is productive.

What I am suggesting in these pages is that we give God a chance too. So, for a few minutes a day, I am asking the reader to check the discursive intelligence at the door—all the itching to see the end, to get it over, to come up with answers, to capture everything in words and formulas. I am asking the reader to take the risk of being vulnerable to God.

Prayerful Moments

The prayerful practices suggested on the following pages will, I hope, be self-explanatory: in the very doing of them, their purpose should become clear. All they intend to do is set up situations where the person praying can become more aware of the presence of God in the moment than he or she would be in ordinary time—caught up in the discursive mode of living or the distressed mode where life's pileups seem to take precedence over life's true meaning. After the suggested situation in the exercise is set up and some instructions are given, the two of you are on your own.

But there are several warnings about these exercises worth making. You will probably discover them for yourself, but there is no harm in anticipating them—even though that act goes against the grain of anti-discursiveness.

First of all, the exercises are not a kind of spiritual cookbook: do this operation, stop, look at the recipe again, do that operation, and so on.

Secondly, any of these exercises can be done alone or in a small prayer group. If you are praying alone, read the suggested exercise over, make a few notes if that kind of thing helps you, understand the progression, and then put the book aside and do it. If you are using the exercises in a small group, one person who knows the progress of the exercise can serve as a leader, and in a very quiet voice, can suggest the next step to the group.

Third, find a place for prayer where you won't be interrupted or distracted. Later on, you may be able to withdraw into the deepest places in yourself with lots of people all around, but to begin, it's best to start as simply and as solitarily as possible.

Even if you are able to sit on top of a flagpole or in a cave in Tibet, however, you will still have distractions: itches, remote noises, even the breeze, but especially from your own regular mind-set and memories: "Oh, I've got to remember to call Edna....Gee, that was a good idea, I must write it down....Boy, if I could only get Harry to have the insight I just got!" There are only two persons who should occupy your focused consciousness while you pray—you and God, and far less of you than of God.

If you are distracted—and you will be—you can gradually learn to catch yourself at it and return to focus on the prayer again. This is one reason why the "trigger" for each prayer session should be simple— no more than a few verses of Scripture, the single word "Jesus," even your own breathing—so that there is a defined center to which you can return.

Fourth, make up your mind when you begin that you're going to sit there for a full fifteen minutes. Put your watch in your pocket and forget the bloody thing. Especially in the beginning, you're going to get antsy; Teresa of Avila used to get up from her knees and shake the hourglass at points to make the time go faster!

But even if it takes a certain quiet discipline to remain still and at peace, keep at it. After a while, if things go reasonably well, you'll have to set an alarm clock to stop you! For all our talk about wanting peace, we find ourselves running pell-mell away from it. But it will grow on you if you give it a chance.

Finally, avoid assessing your progress. Some people suggest keeping a "prayer journal" to log progress and regression, but I personally think such a process is deadly. Prayer ceases to be a sharing of aliveness and becomes an experiment in which I myself am both subject and monitor. Don't stand aloof from yourself and say, "Hmmm. Look at me sitting here," or "Oh, I see! This is what's happening to me!" Far less should you think, "Gasp! What would so-and-so think if she walked in and saw me doing this?" And never, never say, "Oh, well. That was supposed to happen inside me but it didn't."

Strange as it sounds to the discursive mind, you are not at prayer to learn. You are there to meet a Person. You are there to share love. You are there to share aliveness with God.

PRAYING TO BE MORE DEEPLY HUMAN

Aren't we all human already? Well, yes and no.

We don't walk around on our knuckles; we're capable of thinking and reflecting back on our own experience; we can anticipate results, plan, hope, fear the not-yet-existent. We're the only animals who can do these things.

We are all born human, but that humanity is only a *potential*. It needs be activated. Just look at the glazed and vacant eyes of Times Square prostitutes and pushers, mob hit men, terrorists, or serial killers, even subway changemakers. They were born with the same potential for abundant human life as Mother Teresa and Terry Anderson. But no one seems to have told them about it. Or else, activating their humanity took too much effort. Or, more likely, the ambient culture was simply too shrill: "Eat this and become like God!"

Even those of us who try to keep growing as humans are sabotaged by immediate pressures and promises. Like the recognition that we are indeed affected by the force of gravity, our conscious awareness of being human sits way back in the outer reaches of our awareness.

12

Humanity is not something one focuses on too frequently—which is why, I suspect, so many people end up acting inhumanly: losing their tempers, cheating, shredding reputations, accepting fists and guns, and slaughtered children as an unavoidable way of settling differences. Were we to reflect more often on our own humanity and the humanity of everyone we meet, there might be fewer prisons, fewer wars, fewer needless sufferers. Fewer humans would act like beasts.

What separates evolving human beings from animals with an inactivated human potential is conscience. As far as we know, no lion slinks into a village, gobbles up a lamb, then lurches back to its cave moaning, "Oh, God! I did it again! I've got to get some counseling!" But humans do. At least good humans do. Bad humans don't.

What is equally as corrosive, on the rare occasions that we fall back on the term "human," we do so only when we need justification for our own stupidity, as when we bungle and say, "Oh, well, who's not human, right?" Which is like saying that being human means acting stupidly, acting like an unevolved human.

To be fully human—as opposed to childish or animal—is to know who you are and where you are going: a pilgrim with at least a rough map.

Knowing who you are is a matter of sizing up the world around you—the background by which you can see what the world really is and what life expects, with as little distortion as possible and without defensive self-deceptions.

It means being at peace with the unchangeables: your DNA, past mistakes, the family you came from, the personalities of most of the people who populate your life. It also means making an honest assessment of your own self—the talents and limitations, the susceptibilities to fooling yourself, the legitimate expectations you have, and so forth—all the facets of one's body and mind and spirit.

Once you have a calm and clear-eyed grasp of what the world and you yourself seem to be—even if it is only temporary and inadequate—then you can begin choosing from the endless alternative ways of directing that one life you have in your possession. Knowing who you are, you can choose where you are able and want to go.

Extremely few women and men do that. Far too many sort of "fall into" a haphazard and hazy approximation of who they are and what life is for and where they are being dragged and shoved. It could hardly be called a "grasp" on their lives, since that word implies some degree of sureness and control. It is rather more like a "suspicion" or a "vague feeling" about…well, everything.

As a result, such people let life "happen to" them. Like animals, they allow themselves to be shunted and herded here and there, turned away from one path because it's too steep, huddling in fear of the elements and the boss's rages and their peers' expectations. They are far more like sheep than like human beings.

Laying aside for the moment any consideration of God at all, it is my further contention that, even as human beings, such people will never achieve anything remotely like a "grasp" of who they are and where they are going—in a word, of their own humanity—until they make the effort to find some time for peace each day, time to ponder, time to meditate, time to pray.

EXERCISE

Find a quiet spot someplace and sit quietly. Select a spot, if possible, away from the hurly-burly of daily events. Purposefully create an atmosphere of serenity, using whatever means suits your preferences. At the very least, mentally imagine yourself retreating to a corner of your heart that is undistracted and soothing.

Ponder that two-edged question: Who am I, really, and where am I going with my life? Or if that seems too broad, ask yourself the simpler question: Am I really more or less in control of my values, my time, my goals, or is the control really "out of my hands"?

Searching for Simplification

We live in the most complex time in human history. Hurry, bustle, keep it moving, have it on my desk by yesterday! In every free moment, our senses are assaulted by billboards and ads and commercials shouting at us to buy this—or else! It's like being locked up in an asylum for insane carnival hucksters— and yet we've gotten so used to adapting to this sensory bombardment that we rarely realize how numb we have become.

When we get home, the evening news presses our faces into unending human suffering and frustration beamed from all over the world—of which men and women in earlier times were mercifully ignorant— wars here, revolutions there, droughts and famines, starving orphans, kidnappings and rapes, tornadoes and floods. And the implicit question is, "All right. The human family is no longer just a small clan squatting together around a cave or a cabin or a little village. There are five billion people out there, suffering. Are you just going to sit there and watch, or are you going to do something about it?"

Leave me alone!

And all of this comes to us through a smothering, nerve-wrenching blanket of noise—radio, television, compact discs, sirens of police cars and ambulances, airplanes, trains, trucks: noise from people shouting to be noticed. Is there no calm eye in this hurricane of cacophony where one can find peace?

Leave me alone!

16

And someone is always watching, testing us: job evaluations, report cards, efficiency reports, SAT scores, parking meter monitors, tryouts, interviews, promotions. Who's the best? Who has the most money? Who has the biggest biceps? Who's thinnest? Who's playing quarterback? Who gets the raise? Is it any wonder then that so many people, young and old, feel persecuted or even paranoid?

Leave me alone!

And always the rebellious question deep inside: Why? Not merely why must I cater to these peoples' selfishness, power, and prejudice, but why must I knuckle under to "the way things are"? Why do those I love have to suffer? Why doesn't anybody have all the answers?

And here the greatest turmoil boils up: There are so many voices shouting what they *say* are the answers: "It's the materialist system," screams one. "No, it's the rebelliousness of youth," yells another. "Drop out!...Go to Mass!...Take it easy!...Assert your rights!...Do what you're told!"

Leave me alone!

Is that all life is? Working like a dray horse fifty weeks a year for the sake of a crummy two-week vacation? Is the secret just in developing numbness to the intimidating newscasts, the noise, the demands and competitions, the answers that aren't answers at all?

Where's the focus control that will shift this kaleidoscopic complexity into something I can see as a whole, something unified, something with a clear, simple purpose? It's like being spun around until you're dizzy, then opening your eyes in a maze of carnival mirrors.

The answer is simple, at least to say. In fact, it was there, viscerally, all the time: leave me alone.

I am surely not recommending each of us become a hermit—not as a complete way of life. In the first place, it's the rare man or woman who can stand such a total withdrawal; most of us need others. And others need us.

What I'm suggesting is that each of us also *needs*—at the very depths of our humanity—to become a hermit for at least fifteen minutes a day. Unless there is an island of peace and sanity in the excited turmoil of our day, we'll drown in the confusion and complexity and frustration. We'll die as specifically *human* beings.

What does it cost to achieve a measure of peace, focus, simplification in the midst of a busy day? All it costs is—for fifteen minutes a day—letting go.

First of all, one has to realize and accept the unarguable fact that we do indeed need a few minutes a day to achieve perspective. Then one must actually stretch open an empty space in the hurricane of busyness to be alone. (And I am not yet speaking of praying or even realizing the presence of God. I am speaking only of the human need to re-collect one's self.)

Moving from the recognition of the need to that initial decision to take the time, though, is more difficult than I have made it sound. Even though it seems obvious that everyone, young and old, craves simplification and a measure of peace each day, actually taking the steps to achieve it is a whole other ball game. There's just too much else to do, too many "important things." I'd like to, but I just can't seem to find the time.

But is that really true? It's the rare individual who doesn't have at least a little fat in each day: a couple of hours with the television, a half-hour with this one and then that one on the phone, the Saturday basketball game or golf match, the coffee break, the bridge game. There's no doubt we all need time just to relax and "do nothing" with other people.

But why can't we ever carve out fifteen minutes to *really* relax, to do absolutely nothing but re-collect ourselves? "Well, because I just never think about it—and, to tell you the truth, I'm rather afraid of missing something." Right. But if you don't take the time to meet your true self, you really are missing something: you.

If one of the children falls down and gets cut, somebody can find the time to minister to that child's needs, even though it was an unexpected interruption. That's a given; it's more important than anything you were doing at the time. But when you can't take time to assess your own inner hurts, they remain like a low-grade fever, constantly sapping your strength and available emotional energy.

Whenever a mother (inevitably) mentions in confession that she's lost her temper with her children, I always say, "For your penance, take a half-hour every afternoon just before the kids come home, sit in an easy chair with your feet up, with a cup of tea, and just relax." Very often, she gets tears in her eyes. Why? Because it makes such obvious good sense! Rather than rushing around getting "things" ready, the mother should relax and get her *self* ready.

19

What I suggest—not only for mothers, but for stockbrokers and students and steelworkers—is fifteen minutes a day, not to "psych yourself up" but to psych yourself down. This means, only for those few moments, detaching oneself from everything that fluctuates and changes, and tranquilly resting in motionless repose. These moments of repose merely mean sitting in a chair or on the floor, or lying calmly but awake and aware, and letting it all drain out: all the confusion, all the deadlines, all the questions.

Retreat from the bustle and obligation, and merely *be* there in the space—open, emptied, at peace, receptive. It is not the time to try to "solve" anything. It is merely the time to re-collect one's peace and perspective. The solving can wait fifteen minutes—and the man or woman facing a question after a few minutes of peaceful withdrawal will be far more likely to find a truer solution.

It's not the poets and contemplatives who go crazy. It's the "solvers." The man or woman who tries to bring an intensity of intelligence or emotion to a problem usually ends up with teeth gritted so tightly that their fillings fuse together, and their brains along with them.

Life is an infinite sea, G. K. Chesterton said, but the man or woman who tries to "solve" everything is trying to cross the infinite sea, thus witlessly trying to make it finite. The poet and the contemplative float easily on the infinite sea and enjoy the view. They find peace.

EXERCISE

Rather than merely reading about the effects of a few moments of peace, begin to try it.

Find a place where you are pretty sure you won't be disturbed by radios, traffic, people. Put your watch in your pocket or purse.

Sit with your hands resting quietly in your lap. Let yourself relax. Close your eyes and take a deep, deep breath. *Really* deep. Hold it for a second or two, then let it go—and let all the tension go out with it. Roll your head around slowly from shoulder to chest to shoulder until the tension goes out of your muscles. Then let your head sag to your chest.

Let your shoulders sag, and let the tiredness and tension sink down through your back and arms into the chair or floor. Imagine the tiredness like waves of energy draining down through your legs into the floor. Gravity is pulling the gravity out of you.

Just sit there with your mind quiet, letting your imagination travel again through your empty head and down through your empty shoulders and back and chest. If you have to say something to keep the focus of your concentration, just say over and over in the deepest part of yourself, "Peace. Peace." For these few moments, there is nothing to worry about. "Peace."

If you start to feel tension, take another deep breath and exhaust the tension with it.

Read the directions again. It's really quite simple. Just draining out the busy-ness from top to bottom, then resting in that peaceful place.

Now try it.

Seeking Awareness

When you are walking along a busy downtown street, how much do you see of what is going on? Nearly nothing, actually. There are an almost infinite number of stimuli bombarding your senses—people, stores, vehicles, signs—clamoring for attention, and in order to preserve your sanity, you automatically raise up protective shields, a kind of screen that will let only those stimuli pass through which you can tolerate.

The trouble is that our senses are assaulted so often during the day, not just on the streets but in the office, classroom, home, that we keep the shields up even when there is relative calm—like someone with arms raised to ward off a blow, even when we are alone. As a result, we are in danger of losing perception of anything gentle or commonplace. Unless food is burning hot or music earsplitting or colors blistering they have little chance of getting through the shields. Consequently, we are often aware only of the surfaces of life—and only then the most blatantly obvious surfaces at that.

Unless one is in love with another person, who pays attention to the color of his eyes or the part in her hair or the textures of each other's skin? Such attention to the seemingly trivial detail is apparently unimportant; and we end up with only a hazy "picture" of those whom we classify as acquaintances.

But isn't that almost like *really* looking at only one or two people in one's whole life and seeing all the rest with the reception out of focus? And how many potentially fascinating people does that leave tuned out completely? If we were to approach even a few more people with the same intensive awareness with which we approach someone we love ardently, how much would our lives be enriched?

A heightened awareness of the rich facets of life is another "what's-in-it-for-me" benefit arising out of taking the time to meditate. If there is peace in my day into which I can retreat, the rat race slows down, the pressures to hold up the shields ease off. Even a few moments of psychological distance allow things to fall back into their proper sizes.

One day a good friend was grading *Macbeth* tests at his desk at home when his little daughter came up and said, "Daddy, Daddy! Come quick! The roof!

The birds!" But he was up against a deadline; he'd promised his students he'd have the papers back the following day.

With hardly a look, my friend said, "Not now, honey. Daddy's busy." He went on with his work when suddenly he was aware of her still standing by his desk, a fat tear running down her cheek. In that moment, he really saw her.

Wisely, he got up and let her lead him by the hand to the apartment window, and for ten minutes they looked out at the birds on the adjoining roof. They weren't "accomplishing" anything, but something important was happening between father and daughter—an interaction that was irreplaceable.

In that moment of clear vision, things had fallen into their true perspective for him again. *Macbeth* had lasted for three hundred and fifty years; but his daughter would be filled with wonder for only a few.

Robert Frost's poem, "Stopping by Woods on a Snowy Evening," which every schoolchild has heard over and over—and rarely listened to—says the same thing: "The woods are lovely, dark and deep. / But I have promises to keep / And miles to go before I sleep." There is no time to *see* things; only time to *do* things.

William Carlos Williams (a busy city doctor, who still had time to write poetry) also tries to pull us up short and remind us of the important things:

so much depends
    upon
        a red wheel
            barrow
                glazed with rain
                    water
                        beside the white
                            chickens

Not only does taking time to reflect put the outside world into perspective, it also allows us—for a rare moment—to come into contact with the deepest part of our own selves. We become so caught up in the surfaces of ourselves, the things that the ads want us to worry about—lines around the eyes, odors, clothes—that we neglect the deepest places of who-we-are.

The human person is an iceberg with only a fraction of its massive reality protruding at the surface. And it is difficult for us to imagine the enormous power that lurks unsuspected beneath the iron doors that separate our conscious selves from our subconscious selves. And it is in those unprobed depths—those secret, unsuspecting places— that the Spirit of God dwells in us and awaits us.

Limiting our attention still to the purely human sphere, we see a power of spirit deep within each self which we are kept from tapping because of the innumerable calls on our time and on our purely surface awareness. If only we could focus on one surface—like my friend with his little girl—and let its inner truth enter us, perhaps we could turn the same awareness into the deeper parts of ourselves and contact a source of aliveness and serenity that we have been carrying around, unnoticed, all the years of our lives.

EXERCISE

Always begin with the relaxation exercise given earlier in this chapter. Focus on breathing out all the busy-ness and distractions. Find a quiet center.

Step 1. While you are sitting there relaxed and away from the world for a while, hold some kind of natural object on your lap—an orange, a rose, a textured stone—and absorb it with your consciousness. Study its veins and pockmarks, its surface quality and its heft. Give it the full focus of your relaxed receptivity. Then let your imagination roam: Where did it come from? Who has handled it before? What keeps it going?

The purpose of this part of the exercise is not botanical or geological study; the purpose is to focus your relaxed contemplation, your observant attention on this object. Even if you can only manage a few moments, try to heighten your awareness of the facets and fascination of the single natural object in this infinitely faceted world.

Step 2. Then set the object aside and shift your heightened attentiveness to some part of yourself—your hand, your heartbeat, your breathing. Let your attention rest inquiringly on the same physical textures and rhythms as you did with the nonhuman object. Then, quietly, peacefully, dwell on the same questions: Where did this come from? How does it keep me going?

This part of the exercise, too, is not a scientific inquiry but merely an attempt to reflect peacefully on the incredible complexity of this body that carries us about, supplies us with information, shapes our communications with other human beings.

Feeding the Spirit

The human person is not some kind of tripartite complex of three separable blocks: body, mind, and spirit. It is a living intermesh of all three of those realities, and no scientist or philosopher can tell you where the body's functions end and the mind takes over, where the mind and body fall away and the spirit is free to soar beyond the limits of time and space.

And yet each of the three aspects of a human being can be studied by itself, setting aside momentarily the other two, as long as we realize the dependence of each on the others. Surely, the body of a human being has all the properties of any other animal body: it takes up space, moves us from here to there, needs food, oxygen, rest.

The human mind, on the other hand, even though it is dependent on the body and warps to the body's condition, has a measure of control over the body and its functions. What's more, as the body is meant to cope with space, the mind is meant to cope with time: remembering, recognizing, making judgments, computing, planning, and so forth. Its processes are localizable in the human brain.

But there are other activities of the human person that, though dependent on the body and mind, do not seem to be strictly limited to them or by them. There is some aspect of the human person that seems able to work even *counter* to the mind and its logic.

We see this antilogic when someone falls in love. Why care so crazily about this person? Why *this* person and not another? And that love cannot find full expression through either the body or the mind. It is in this area of human activity that we "hope against hope," that we trust one another, that we rejoice, cope with mystery, feel the wonder and ecstasy that lets us swing free of body and mind. These are the kinds of human activities—it seems to me—these higher-order activities that the present world is slowly, witlessly, starving to death.

The human body feeds on the bodies of other animals, the vegetation of the earth, air, sunshine, and so forth. The human mind feeds on information, the evidence passed on by the bodily sensors, the experiences other men and women compress into words and share with us.

And just as the body's sensors feed the mind, the products of the body-mind feed the spirit. But the sometimes inscrutable activities of the spirit—love, hope, faith, mystery—are beyond the scope of either body or mind. Love, hope, faith, and mystery cannot be boxed in by logic or by weighing or measuring or timing. When the spirit is active, it is to some extent able to leap free of time and space, free of body and mind.

When the body is hungry, it lets us know, and it grunts and gurgles tyrannically until we feed it. The hungers of the human mind flicker when our sense of curiosity is aroused—the itch to know, to uncover, to see behind the closed door.

But the demands of the mind are more easily avoided than the demands of the body: inertia very often puts the book back on the shelf unread, moves the finger out of the dictionary, reaches for the buttons of the television or the computer, and contents itself with passively ingesting mental baby food.

The body gurgles; the mind itches; but the hunger of the spirit expresses itself in restlessness and discontent—a discontent that is often very vague and formless. It is not as easy to deal with the hunger of the spirit as it is to pin down the rumblings of the belly or the curiosity of the mind.

The body can shift position when it is uncomfortable; the mind can sit with a book or a pencil or a teacher. But the restlessness of the spirit usually arises in questions for which there seem to be no cut-and-dried answers: Why doesn't she love me? Why do I fail even when I try my best? What's it all about? The human spirit feeds on peace and joy—and there seems precious little of either in our world today.

In the hurly-burly of work and noise, where can the human spirit find peace? In the indifferent, plastic, and numbing routine, where can the human spirit find joy? The love of a few close friends gives some measure of both, but it is so transitory, so infrequent, that the spirit is in danger of withering and leaving the human person to be little more than a computer carried around by a hundred pounds or so of sensitive flesh.

Many people feed this hunger of the spirit with art. For those who understand and are willing to take the time, the moments spent absorbing a painting in a museum or watching bodies dance or drinking in the music of a concert or sharing the life of a novel are moments that uplift the spirit and feed its hunger for peace and joy.

🌿
30

The arts are not in any sense "useful." They cannot be weighed or counted; they cannot be stored away as so much purposeful information. Although the paintings themselves or the theater tickets or the books can be sold and bought, the experiences of them are not acts of commerce. And yet their effect is obvious in the placidity of those men and women who are able to absorb themselves and be at rest in them. Their spirits are enlivened.

EXERCISE

Begin with the deep-breathing, relaxation exercise given earlier in this chapter. Use the first few moments to clear your mind and relax your body. Let the world slip away.

Step 1. Take a book like Edward Steichen's *Family of Man* or *Life Magazine*'s year-end issue or the collected works of any photographer specializing in recording the human condition. Select a picture which shows human beings caught at special moments of being uniquely human. Pore slowly over the picture, without any hurry to "get through" or to "understand," absorbing yourself in the photograph and its inhabitants for as long as the picture still feeds your spirit. Try to know the people portrayed—their pain, their joy, their true humanness.

Continue selecting additional photographs, as long as this exercise still "feeds" your spirit.

Step 2. From the photographs you have chosen, pick one person who seems to speak most eloquently to you. Connect with the part of the person who might be most closely related to your own feelings and spirit. Relax and empathize with that person and your similarities.

🌿
31

The same kind of restful absorption and empathy with others can take place, surprisingly, in the most peace-less of places—a busy street corner or the lobby of a hotel or an airport lounge. Merely sit quietly, as if you were invisible, and watch the faces, the ways that personalities express themselves in movements and reactions, the hundreds of human lives that are filled with their private joys and sorrows—as is yours.

Finding Wisdom

There is, as most people know, a qualitative difference between knowledge and wisdom. The two are surely related: wisdom has something to do with what you know, but it goes much further. When you have a problem for which there is a clear-cut answer—"How much do I have to pay in taxes? What makes thunder and lightning? Where are my cufflinks?"—you go to someone, an expert, who has knowledge.

But when you've got a mystery on your hands, a question for which there is no apparent answer— "What's it all about? Where is everything going? Why did my child die?"—you need someone with wisdom. Any competent physician has the knowledge to explain the causes of your child's death; far fewer are able to explore with you the *reasons why* anyone has to die.

Anyone can accumulate facts if he or she has patience and a retentive memory. This ability of the mind is like a computer: taking in and storing data, manipulating it logically, and coming up with answers. But this juncture between knowledge and wisdom is precisely where the mind and the spirit differ. Knowledge and logic are qualities of the mind; wisdom is a quality of the spirit.

Pause and think of someone whom you believe to be wise. Usually it is someone a bit older. Wisdom has something to do with experience, with having lived a bit. But all older people are not wise; accumulating experiences isn't the only element of wisdom. Neither, necessarily, is the number of books one has read. There is a quality about a wise person that has nothing to do with *quantity* at all. There is a sense that the person has assimilated the meaning of these experiences and books, grasped its inner core, made it a part of the self.

33

The reasons one feels confident in listening to this person's advice is that the wise man or woman has a kind of assurance, a calm and peaceful *possession* of the truth and can discern more clearly and judge more soundly what is true or false, what is right or wrong, what is truly important or unimportant, what will lead to joy or what will lead to self-destruction.

The person of knowledge wants definite answers and is angry at uncertainty; the person of wisdom is searching, too, but that person seems made far less fearful or upset by uncertainty. Perhaps that is one sure hallmark of wisdom: being at peace with the unchangeable and the unfathomable.

Wisdom has something to do with experience *reflected upon*. But if one is too busy doing and experiencing to have time for quiet reflection, then life becomes not a connected whole—understood and accepted—but merely one-damn-thing-after-another.

Such people—most people—endure the intermittent sufferings of their lives with the dumb incomprehension of animals: weeping, gnashing teeth, crying tormentedly. "Why me?" The wise man or woman has achieved a certain perspective not only on the suffering of others but on their own. Because they have taken the time and the effort—and pain—to face the sufferings of life rather than run from them, they understand more clearly that suffering is unavoidable.

They understand, too, that there are some unpleasant facts of life that neither they, for all their efforts, nor science, for all its studies, nor prayers, nor groaning, nor rebellion will ever uproot or change. The fact of life is that the child born deformed cannot be restored to total normalcy; he or she can only be loved. The alcoholic cannot be convinced—at least now—by all the arguments in the world; he or she can only be loved, reminded, refused the victory of ruining others' lives. The spendthrift cannot be taught budgeting and caution; he or she can only be loved, tolerated, challenged, allowed to hurt until they get some measure of wisdom or not.

The wise person knows that all our progress will never make evil go away. There will always be unkindness and selfishness and death. That is the way things are.

In a word, the wise person knows that there is no god but God. Science is not God. Progress is not God. Money is not God. And, most important, the wise person knows that he or she is not God.

That sounds rather silly. We all know our shortcomings; we all know we are not God. But do we? Don't our actions—the grunting and groaning, the yearning for perfection in ourselves and others, the search for the answers when nothing more can be done—don't these actions really belie our claims that we are not God? Don't they really say, "I can find the answer, even if there isn't one! I *won't* accept the fact that I am limited!"

In accepting the inevitable, the unchangeable, the wise person accepts the true perspective of things, his or her position in the ascending order of beings in the universe. The wise person knows that he or she is better than a rock or a rutabaga or an orangutan. But he or she is less than God.

It is surprising how much less such people seem to suffer. At times, the wise person seems almost callous—refusing to sob or screech or swear revenge on the universe. Instead, wise people ride out the storm with a kind of placid detachment which seems, to the insensitive, to be insensitivity. It is not that at all.

It is like—on a much more mundane level—the person who goes to the dentist, sits back and says, "I know from experience that this is going to hurt. Okay. But I also know from experience that I can get through the pain."

Somehow such a person actually experiences less physical pain than one who tenses up, tightens, as if there were some way he or she could cringe away from the unavoidable pain. The same thing occurs in childbirth when the expectant mother has been schooled to expect—and accept—a degree of pain in labor. But for the mother all tensed up and ready to defend herself, fear multiplies the actual pain a hundredfold.

The analogy can extend, I think, to any pain at all—feeling unwanted, failing at a job, losing a loved one. The wise man or woman struggles to avoid pain, but when it is demonstrably unavoidable, he or she says, "This will hurt, but I will endure." As a result, they suffer less than those who whine or rage and shake their fists at the silent sky, shouting, "How can a good God do this to me?" As if they expected an answer.

Wisdom does *not* come from suffering. If it did, animals in experimental laboratories would be wiser than all of us. Wisdom comes from suffering reflected upon, accepted, and assimilated. The wise person does not have "solutions" to suffering, but such people do know what the truths of human life are. Somehow they have used reflectiveness not only to heal their minds but actually to take their suffering and turn it into their strength.

But without time to put suffering into perspective, the self will be dominated by the slings and arrows of outrageous fortune that assault us all from the outside and the civil war between the parent and the child inside. If one is to achieve self-possession, if one is to achieve wisdom, he or she must first conquer the need to rush around constantly, to escape from the facts of human life. Each of us must take time to withdraw from the transitory in order to discover the permanent.

EXERCISE

Begin with the usual deep-breathing, using your breathing to find a centered spot far removed from distractions and distempers of daily life.

Step 1. Focus your attention on some problem you have—a feeling of inadequacy, a constant weakness, some kind of lack or loss—or on a really stupid and hurtful mistake you have made. Then when the feelings about this personal focus you have chosen become really intense, *repeat* the relaxing exercise.

Step 2. Then take a book of photographs such as Steichen's *Family of Man* or *Life Magazine*'s best photographs and, in that quiet, meditative mood, turn the pages slowly until you come to a painful picture that holds your attention. Pore over it, absorb yourself into it. Then, with this event still filling your inner self, quietly compare your original problem with this problem. Very calmly put the two events—your problem and this catastrophe—into comparison and perspective.

Instead of being just a spectator or arm's length observer of this photograph, create compassion with the person or persons in the photo. You may not actually have much experience with the topic of the photograph, but the picture can provide a vicarious experience that your imagination can make into a very real part of your own being.

Pursuing Authentic Freedom

Most people who don't think deeply or often believe that true freedom means the ability to do absolutely anything one wants, without restriction—even without the restriction of the action's natural consequences. And they yearn for that kind of freedom, ache inwardly and endlessly for it.

To put it concretely, this quest for false freedom often means that such people want to be so rich that they can get away with anything. Their hearts rebel against the petty but tyrannous demands of the book, the teacher, the spouse, the parent. They grind their teeth at the unfairness of things—that the wicked prosper while the honest go hungry, that the rich, the beautiful, the charming, the talented, the degreed are fawned over and rewarded while the flawed—most of us—find condescension or ostracism, as the beautiful pass on to someone more interesting.

But few of us will ever be so rich that people will not be free to refuse us their love. They may pander to our desires in order to collect their pay, but we cannot buy their inner acceptance with money. If such were the case, there would be only one person free and all the rest would be slaves—not only externally but internally too. If someone were to achieve that power, it would be a "gift" as deadly as that given to King Midas. When love is not freely given, it is no longer love.

Actually, the content of the idea of "freedom" which such people vaguely envision and long for seems not really the desire to be free but the desire to be sovereign—with no higher power than oneself, with nothing above in any form that might hinder them in any way or tie them down.

Good luck. That is manifestly impossible—even for kings, even for billionaires, divas, sultans, and empresses.

Even Ghengis Khan was *subject* to the law of gravity. He had to submit, as humbly as a slave, before windstorms, earthquakes, and floods. Whether he wanted to or not, he had to eat, sleep, suffer toothaches, grow weary. There was a limit to how much he could drink without passing out or getting sick. He was locked into *that* time and *that* place and *that* self. If one were empress of all the world, with all the money and all the power, she would still be as powerless as a peasant in the face of death.

So often people say, "If only I'd been born at that time," or "If only my parents had been such-and-such." Those two words—"If only"—are the two most wasted words known to humankind, since whatever follows them is always utterly impossible. Yet how subtly but deeply we are enslaved to those impossible words.

All right. So everyone will grant, in their saner moments, there are certain things over which no human being is sovereign. What we really mean, then, is that we wish we could be free of criticism, free of the demands and expectations of others. Most people are too subject to what others think of them but, unless you are willing to go off and be a hermit, you will never be free of criticism or demands or expectations.

To live in any society—that of Nazi Germany or of a Waco commune, that of an ordinary family or a society of Hell's Angels—means automatically to set up a web of relationships or interlocking expectations and responsibilities. Even two people alone on a desert island have their freedom limited by the fact that another depends on them. Either one of them may not like it, but that's the way things are. Either one is free to kill off the other, but the inescapable consequence (from which he or she is *not* free) is to live alone.

To love is automatically to surrender a part of one's freedom to the beloved, who can call on one's time or effort and concern even when it is completely inconvenient.

Freedom, then, is not the ability to be untouched by the pressures that a physical life on earth imposes on all of us, from peasant to president. Nor does it mean being untouched by the limitations that living together imposes on all of us, from New Ager to Hitler. True freedom comes from knowing and accepting the truth—the way things really are—no matter how unpleasant, and acting accordingly with complete peace of mind.

For such a desirable reality, you can define freedom only in negatives; *not* bound, *without* restrictions, *un*controlled. And such words describe a state of freedom from *external* limitation—like gravity and report cards and tax notices and prison bars. But the real freedom, the freedom that can survive any external limitation—even solitary, even death—is *internal* freedom.

A man or woman can be forced by external pressure to get up at a certain hour, do such and such unpleasant work, forgo the fulfillment of dreams, put on a happy face. But inside, he or she is still free to think and believe whatever he or she wishes.

A man or woman is also free to stand up against those external pressures whenever he or she chooses freely to do so—provided he or she is at peace with the inevitable consequences. You can stand up and tell the boss to go to hell, but then you have to pay the piper. You can refuse to tell secrets even under torture, but the alternative is that the torture will get worse. You can sell all you have and give it to the poor, but you will have to get along without a washer and a dryer and a portable cassette player.

Granted there are restrictions on all of us, it is astonishing that people so rarely use the freedom they actually *do* have. It is pitiful how much undeserved abuse we will take when we have the freedom to say "Stop!" It is silly how many hours we neutralize our powers in front the television when we are free to do so many other things.

But is that quite true? In a sense, the couch potato is free to go for a walk, paint a picture, go to a ball game, mow the lawn, pray—or a hundred thousand other things.

But is he or she *really* free? Where I teach, whenever a student has a "free" period, he can do any number of profitable things to justify his parents' sacrifice to pay his tuition. But nearly every one of them heads for the cafeteria to shoot the breeze—with all the "freedom" of iron filings in front of a magnet. Many of us, often during the day, are free *from* any external demand. The question is whether we are free *to* do anything other than the habitual things. Freedom-from is not automatically freedom-to.

Again, freedom is ironic. It is like money in your pocket, nice to know you have, but worthless until you *spend* it on something you want more than the money. Freedom comes into play only when you commit yourself to a single choice—thus, at least momentarily, *giving up* your freedom to choose the other options.

In order to be free from our own self-imposed limitations, we must first be aware that there are actually alternatives and have some idea what each of those alternatives will cost. I have to laugh when I hear young people angrily demanding, "I want to be free to be who I *am*!" But when I reply, "Of course you do. But who *are* you?" They usually slump and grump, "I dunno." Freedom is most often curtailed by our own ignorance.

I suspect one of the reasons we become so addicted to our habits is that they make things so much easier. We don't have to think at all of what else we could more profitably—and more happily—be doing. If the television is sitting there, the only real choice is which program we want to bore ourselves with.

Calculated ignorance of alternatives minimizes one's freedom not only in trivial situations, such as how to spend a couple of "free" hours, but also in crucial situations, such as which spouse to choose, which college to choose, which line of work to choose, which religion to choose. If a girl, for instance, knows of only one or two colleges, or if a boy really knows only one girl, their freedom is scaled down to the absolute minimum. The less you know, the less confused you are—but the less likely to be free. You are not free to choose an alternative—no matter how beautiful or fulfilling—if you haven't taken the trouble to discover that it even exists.

Furthermore, when one justifies a so-called "choice" with such statements as "Oh, well, everybody cheats" or "That's what everybody says," there is no genuine freedom there at all. Those "choices" are enslaved to "everybody."

When I see seniors go off to college, I realize that they will be free to go to bed with anyone willing, stop going to Mass, and get drunk as long as the money holds out. But how many of them will be truly free—from the external pressures of their peers and from the inner pressures of their own need to belong, to stay chaste, to go to Mass, to enjoy beer without giving up their freedom to it.

The best synonym for "free" might be "unbiased." To make a truly free choice, one must be unbiased by external pressures and unbiased by an ignorance of the alternatives (and the consequences of each). But most importantly, one must be unbiased by the subtle weight of internal pressures: irrational prejudices, previous habits, self-protectiveness, fear of losing what one possesses now in the hope of some not-so-sure benefit in the future.

All those internal obstacles to truly free choice boil down to fear. "But what will happen to me if…?" It becomes like standing on the edge of an icy pool on a hot day. No one is going to push me in. I know how good it will feel after the initial shock. "Okay, here I come. One…two…seventy-six…."

How do we exorcise those irrational attachments that prevent us from making a free choice? The answer is logically simple: we detach ourselves from them. Sounds easy. We all know, though, that it is not.

In his little book of retreat meditations, *The Spiritual Exercises*, Saint Ignatius Loyola says that the only way to shed our predispositions for the easier—or even more debilitating but enjoyable—alternatives is to become "indifferent." By that he means choose the alternative which is the truth—that is, which is the will of God, written right into the natures of human beings and human interactions, which we can read by their nearly inevitable results.

We are free to treat gin like ginger ale, but sooner or later the God-programmed nature of alcohol and the God-programmed nature of the human liver are going to tell us we were wrong. In every decision, choose the truth—no matter what the good or bad consequences to oneself.

This choosing the truth, however, presumes, of course, that one realizes that the universe revolves around God and not around oneself. It presumes that

one understands that the relative merits of one choice
or another choice depend on the way things really
are and not on the way I personally would like them
to be.

45

This "detachment" or "indifference" does not im-
ply that a person becomes insensitive; actually it means
that one becomes *more* acutely sensitive to the truth
lurking below the immediately appealing or repellent
surfaces. Nor does it mean that one must become heed-
less of the way this decision will affect others; in fact,
very often putting one's own self-protectiveness aside
reveals for the first time how the more difficult choice
for oneself will be the better choice for others. "Detachment" means that one chooses without possessive-
ness, without self-serving, without impulsiveness, without greed. It wants to do only the truth.

The best way to make a difficult choice is to bring
yourself to look at the options as if it were someone
else's problem.

Saint Ignatius has exercises intended to show
retreatants what detachment and true freedom really
mean—even if they may not (like the rich young man
in the gospel) be able actually to choose the better
option.

EXERCISE

Perform the usual deep-breathing relaxation exercise, at the same time trying to focus your consciousness not merely on the inner center of yourself but on the Spirit who dwells within you at that most central place.

Step 1. Imagine that through some perfectly honorable means such as a will or a state lottery you have come into $10,000. The money has been delivered to your house in cash. Feel it with your hands: one hundred $100 bills. Weigh it. Feel the texture of it.

Step 2. Think of all you could do with this money. Explore them all, even writing the options out on paper. First decision: Will you use the money all or in part for yourself? What will you buy for yourself? What will you use it to pay for? Second decision: Will you use the money in part or totally for others? If so, for whom? And how far will that circle of generosity extend: just to family, close friends, even strangers?

Remember: to be detached from prejudice, you must not be swayed by selfishness. On the other hand, you must not be uncritically swayed by feeling guilty about spending money on yourself. Money is neither evil nor good; only the use of it is one or the other.

Step 3. Now, in your imagination, see your-self taking the entire bundle of bills in your hands again. Feel them. Now, see if you can picture your-self taking the stack of bills and placing them on the altar in front of the tabernacle. See if you can picture yourself backing away and saying to God, "Okay. What is the *best* choice? What way will using this money accord with the way *you* see things?"

Step 4. Rest there a moment—looking from some distance at the pile of bills resting in front of the tabernacle. What are your inner feelings—in your gut, in your hands? How truly free are you?

Step 5. Evaluate how you would feel in the pre-vious step in the light of this quote:

[Jesus] said also to the one who had invited him, "When you give a luncheon or a dinner, do not invite your friends or your brothers or your rela-tives or rich neighbors, in case they may invite you in return, and you would be repaid. But when you give a banquet, invite the poor, the crippled, the lame, and the blind. And you will be blessed, be-cause they cannot repay you, for you will be repaid at the resurrection of the righteous."

Luke 14:12-14

PRAYING TO ENCOUNTER THE DIVINE

We can humanize ourselves: that is, we can enrich, deepen, intensify our possession of all that it is to be human, if we are willing only to take time to reflect on and challenge our human potential. But we cannot divinize ourselves. Roman emperors tried, with disastrous results. Some people in mental hospitals sadly convince themselves that they are Jesus or Buddha, but no one pauses to worship them.

The very idea of a human being becoming godlike is as unthinkable as a rock taking the notion to walk around or a turnip belting out "The Star-Spangled Banner" or a monkey typing a rough draft of *War and Peace*. No individual on the scale of beings—mineral, vegetable, animal, human—can hoist itself up by its bootstraps onto the next higher level of sensitivity and activity.

But the word is out that a man named Jesus Christ did that for us. As the story goes, the Son of God—limitless, immortal, unhindered by time and space—surrendered all that to become human. He did it in order to let us know that, through him, we could become divinized: the sons and daughters of almighty God.

That is the Good News of the Christian gospel: that we need not fear annihilation at death, that he and his Father are willing to share their Spirit with us, now, if we are willing to receive the gift. In Christ we can become godlike. There is no bootstrap effort on our part to cause this divinization. All we need to do is to recognize the gift and *accept* it.

Like all gifts, the gift of divinization can be refused and therefore, for that individual, "it doesn't work." But the heartbreaking part of such refusals is that the gift of a share in the aliveness of God is usually rejected without the potential receiver even looking it over seriously.

It's like the woman whose rich great-aunt died and left her nothing more than a boring old piece of furniture. Angry at being cheated when she expected so much more, she pitched the dumb thing out without appraising it, without realizing it was an antique worth a fortune. Similarly, many of us were led to expect far more of religion than what we seem to have gotten: catechism answers to meaningless questions, moral strictures, and an hour of repetitive, stultifying ritual every weekend. So, angry at being cheated, many of us pitch out the whole "God thing" without even appraising it, without realizing its price-less worth.

Part of the reason for this sad self-impoverishment is that appraising anything takes a bit of effort and time—not much, but more than we are willing to take from the headlong rush. What's more, if one hasn't made the effort to become even a fully evolved human, he or she will not even be able to see that being Christianized and divinized actually is a value. They will be too contentedly locked into the plastic place-bos of the television and compact disc player. And so they fumble around in what they realize are tiny lives, as oblivious to their own possible greatness as the young Helen Keller was of hers.

Embracing Wide-Angle Vision

We have already seen that as human beings we tend to pull back for security into far too tiny, far too self-centered lives. Without a realization of the im-mensity of the world and its sufferings, our own little sufferings tend to get inflated out of proportion, as-suming an importance and intensity far beyond their causes. But when one sees them in the perspective of the savagery of ethnic wars around the world and the starvation in the countries in sub-Saharan Africa, our own little headaches and disappointments can't help but assume their true size. Our pains and prob-lems are very real, of course, but they are far less dramatic than they seemed when our focus was on our own little cocoons rather than on the wide-angle context of the whole human family.

Imagine, then, how much less significant they can become when seen against the background of all human history, and even less against the background of our own immortality and the endless dimension of God. When the old monks went to their superior with some petty complaint or some bickering difference of opinion, the wise prior would often say, *Quid ad aeternitatem.* Essentially, this Latin aphorism means, "What significance has this event when it is seen in the light of the endless and eternal lifetime Christ won for us?"

Such a realization is dangerous, however.

It is undeniably true that being turned down for a date or missing out on this promotion or even the death of a loved one diminishes to near-insignificance when seen in the context of all the people who have died in the world today, or all the people who have died since the world began, or the eternal life that death cannot end.

Still, such a realization can convince one that nothing he or she does has any objective meaning at all in the long run, that they are—to all intents and purposes—utterly negligible against that enormous background. In a sense, this conclusion is absolutely true and unavoidable. But in another sense, it is not true at all.

The Good News of Christianity does force us to see ourselves as infinitesimally small, like a single drop in an endless ocean of reality. And yet it also says something startlingly contrary to that: despite our insignificance, the God of the Universe—for reasons only God can fathom—finds each of us incredibly important, important enough to send the only-begotten Son to die and rise in order to show us just how precious we are.

As the gospel says, God calls each of us by name; if God cares for the lilies of the field, how much more does the triune God care for us; like a Good Shepherd, God is willing to leave the ninety-nine and come searching for the one who is lost. Now *there* is News to be reckoned with!

We are, on the one hand, lost in the anonymity of billions upon billions of people who have lived here, and we are lost in the endless carouse of the universe. But on the other hand, we stand out, unique, in the eyes of the limitlessly loving Father.

In looking beyond our parochial little neighborhoods, we see that the immensity of the universe is all one. The atoms that make up fire and mountains, cabbages and tigers, asteroids and suns, are the same atoms which weave the web of our selves. You take them into you in food and air; you expel them and they return to the one Whole. We all share the same "stuff" in our makeup and in our continuance.

And yet in the eyes of God, you are an identifiable part of this immense universe. Whole, unique. Someone whose name God knows. Someone whom God will always recognize.

53

EXERCISE

Do the deep-breathing, relaxation exercise first, but end with a realization that in that still center point of yourself, you verge into the presence of God.

Step 1. Sit in this peaceful quietude before a lighted candle. Absorb yourself into the flame calmly, focusing all your attention on the light. If you haven't got a candle, close your eyes and imagine a circle of light with a point of intensity in the middle of it.

Let your imagination "draw" a circle around the point of light, and then let the candle flame or the light point expand in your imagination to fill the circle around it. (It isn't easy, so don't try to rush it.)

When the light has filled the circle, let it contract very slowly again into a point. Then very slowly let it swell out to fill the circle again. The light is like the invisible-but-present atoms that bond the air and the flame and the candle together.

Step 2. Slowly let this light spread out beyond the imaginary circle and fill the room or space you are in. Let it penetrate and fill your body and your mind. Let your whole self be absorbed into the light. (This, too, may take time. Don't try to rush. Don't go on until you feel deep in yourself this union, this being-filled-with the light.) Rest in that awhile.

Step 3. Then let your imagination expand the light from this room and yourself—first out over the whole building, then the whole city, the whole country, the whole globe. Rest in that awhile, knowing that you are a part of this greatness of light.

Step 4. Let your imagination swell out even further as the light spreads out into the whole universe—this immensity of union, bonded piece-to-piece by the light. See both the limitless expanse of the light but also the focus of it emanating from you in this room with this candle. Rest in that realization for as long as it contents you, as long as something is "happening."

Step 5. Finally, let the light break through the barriers of time and space into the immeasurable Light who is the Source of our light, of our shared existence. See in your imagination the widening circles of light from this candle, from yourself, this world, this universe, out into the endless depths of God. Rest easily in that infinite sea of light, knowing you are fused with it and yet not absorbed—still a self, a droplet-point in that endless sea of existence.

If you wish, reread the suggested directions and try this exercise several days in a row. Don't have any expectations. Each time you enter the light, do it peacefully, calmly, easily.

Plumbing the Vitality Beneath Everything

I have a rather well-founded suspicion that the reason many people experiment with drugs is that they *know* there must be a greater aliveness lurking beneath the seemingly impenetrable surfaces of things. Surely there's more to life than the plastic throwaways we spend our hard-earned pennies for. Surely there's more excitement and joy—and even pain—hiding behind the everyday masks of indifference on the people we elbow past on our way to where?

I feel rumblings in the depths of my own self which tell me even the surface self I've settled for is sitting on a volcano of aliveness within me, which I am afraid to see and rejoice in and liberate. A time of contemplative quiet would put me into at least a tentative contact with that powerful aliveness beneath the surfaces of myself and other people and the whole universe. But taking meditative time is repugnant to one always in a rush, and I find it easier to plunk down a few bucks for chemical shortcuts. Even these chemical shortcuts are mere props for a surface life—tickets to a "paradise" of false solutions.

People experienced in meditation have discovered they can indeed penetrate beneath surfaces without chemical keys. Moreover, they can also discover not just disparate and ununified images but a *wholeness* to that powerful subsurface aliveness of which each of us is a part. Even more, they find that this sense of wholeness remains even after the "high" itself has passed.

Gerard Manley Hopkins, the Jesuit poet, summed up what he saw of this inner life in a poem. To some, it could seem merely an ecological poem about human indifference to the destruction of the world. It is, however, intricate and revealing. In itself, it is a fit subject for a mediation.

Read over each line of this poem carefully. Do not move on to the next line or thought until you have absorbed that one.

GOD'S GRANDEUR

The world is charged with the
    grandeur of God.
        It will flame out, like shining from
            shook foil;
        It gathers to a greatness, like the ooze
            of oil
Crushed. Why do men then now not
    reck his rod?
Generations have trod, have trod, have trod;
    And all is seared with trade; bleared,
        smeared with toil;
    And wears man's smudge and shares
        man's smell; the soil
Is bare now, nor can foot feel, being shod.

And for all this, nature is never spent;
There lives the dearest freshness
    deep down things;
And though the last lights off the
        black West went
        Oh, morning, at the brown brink
            eastward, springs—
Because the Holy Ghost over the bent
    World broods with warm breast and
    with ah! bright wings.

It is that "freshness deep down things" that we seek. We are not merely joined together by the impersonal atoms. We are joined to one another, and to our universe, by a shared aliveness, like an underground spring of water from which everything draws its existence. That "freshness," that aliveness, that spring—is the living God.

Halfway around the world from Hopkins and from a totally different culture, the same discovery came along the seemingly same meditative path to a modern Indian writer.

This poet's realization of the aliveness that pulses through me and through every living thing—and through God himself—at one time both liberates me from my tiny isolation and involves me "in that ceaseless ebb and flow of the undulating worldwide sea." Alone, I am limited; in union with this aliveness, I am limitless.

I have paraphrased this seeker's words and put
them into "poetic" lines.

THE PULSE OF GOD

The vitality that flows in waves,
night and day through every vein of my body
flows out to conquer the universe.
It pulsates through the world
in amazing rhythms and cadence;
inspires every pore of the earth's soil
with the thrill of a million
grass-blades growing;
blossoms into flowers and young leaves;
sways, year after year,
in the ceaseless ebb and flow
of the undulating worldwide
sea of life and death.

EXERCISE

Begin by relaxing. Let yourself go. Let all of the problems and challenges of the world and its clocks and deadlines and expectations evaporate. Practice the deep-breathing method outlined earlier.

Step 1. Let your breathing become regular, re-laxed, slowed down. Concentrate your attention just on your own breathing, feeling it, being ab-sorbed in it. Imagine that air is something visible to your imagination, drawn in from outside, held, and filling your body with oxygen, pumping your lungs, feeding your heart and blood—and then being exhaled and returned to our common at-mosphere to be used by others. Repeat this con-sideration for as long as it keeps yielding up more and more: drawn in, working and being used, ex-haled again to be shared.

Step 2. Let your imagination spread, understand-ing that this air you have used and passed on has been used by others in this place, in this town. Where did it come from? In whom has it sustained its life before you? Rest there, understanding, con-templating this truth of the air we all share.

Step 3. The envelope of air encircles the globe, moving restlessly across its face, from Asia to Cali-fornia, to Maine, to Europe, to Asia, to California, in an endless return. It carries storms, rain, snow. It stirs up the sands of the deserts and the waves of the sea. It wafts pollen from plant to plant. The trees absorb its carbon dioxide and give off oxygen to animals and humans, and in the process make food for us. The air feeds fires. It is our common environment; we use it, pass it on, share it. Rest there, with your breathing self at the focus of this enlivening environment of air, breathing it in and out, in and out.

Step 4. The Hebrew word for air or breath is *ruah*. It is the word Scripture uses not only for the atmosphere we breathe but also for the Holy Spirit. The Holy Spirit is the living breath. Resting in the physical air you are breathing in and out, think of . this wider scope of the breath that sustains us: the spirit of God at creation hovering over the primeval waters " with warm breast and with ah! bright wings"; Yahweh fashioning Adam and "breathing into his nostrils a breath of life" which made him a living human being; the whirlwind and tongues of fire with which the spirit of God visited the Twelve on Pentecost and made them alive with the aliveness of God.

Step 5. Rest there in that life-giving air, breathing it into your lungs, drawing the spirit into your self, surrounded by it, sustained by it, sharing it. Peaceful. Enlivened. Aware.

Journey to Wonder

If the last two meditative exercises have given you some thought, you are quite likely at the edge of some real awareness of the presence of God within you and all around you. Most of us know *about* God, but far fewer know *God*.

As a person, you can find out a certain amount about God from textbooks, just as textbooks and articles can yield a certain amount of information about any famous living person. But reading a biography—or even the Scriptures—is nothing at all compared to the actual experience of finding yourself in the person's immediate presence.

Such "preliminary research for an interview" (which is about all most religious education attempts) is as necessary but ultimately disposable as the first stage of a space rocket. At that point of real ignition, real encounter, the Person takes over and makes all the descriptions look like shadows.

Once one has personally encountered the Guest of Honor, the Mass is no longer merely the same old, deadly, liturgical routine. A short passage of Scripture which describes Yahweh or Jesus is no longer a dry statement about a stranger but of Someone we have encountered for ourselves.

Even the Our Father, which we piously rolled off our tongues as children with no more involvement than we had for reciting our multiplication tables or mouthing familiar nursery rhymes, now takes on a new life when one slowly ponders it phrase by phrase. It is no longer a matter of memory; it is a moment of meeting.

It seems inconceivable that this God of unutterable light, this Spirit of divine aliveness is within me, enlivening, divinizing me at the core of my humanity. And yet it is true. To ask why it is a waste of time, just as it is a waste of time to ask why my friends still love me.

The fact is there. Don't try to analyze it; revel in it! Enjoy it! Sing it! It is equally silly trying to analyze *how* this immeasurable God could permeate the whole universe and yet still be aware of me, focus into me. The fact is there. Dance!

That does not mean this divinely enlivening presence in and around me—like the atoms and air and light—cannot be pondered. But it should be not something dissected by human reason but gazed at and enjoyed by the human spirit—as all love must be. This is a mystery to be wondered at, not a problem to be solved.

God is an infinite sea, and one can only float blissfully on that sea and marvel at the sure safety of a flotation device amid the storms of everyday life. Contemplating God all around me and within me is not a way to find answers; it is a way to find joy.

EXERCISE

This exercise is based on the famous "Jesus Prayer," which may be familiar to some from J.D. Salinger's novel *Franny & Zooey*.

Step 1. Relax. Let go of the world's busy-ness. Breathe deeply, hold it, and let it out with a complete exhaustion of the tensions. Then gradually begin to regulate your breathing. Inhale for a count of five, exhale for a count of five. Try to make the counting gradually slower and slower until it is rhythmic and steady. Let it happen for a while until you are comfortable with it and no longer have to count.

Step 2. Then gradually and very quietly, as you inhale, say in the deepest part of yourself, "Jesus." Then on the exhale, "Somehow you are alive in me." Say this phrase over and over and over, resting in it, drawing aliveness and realization from it.

It needn't be those words. As we will see later with Zen mantras, the words are less important than the rhythm, their ability to focus one's consciousness. But, unlike the Eastern contemplative, the Western mind is trained to demand some content, at least at the beginning of meditating. The reason I chose those words was that they mention Jesus, who is our link to the aliveness of God, the Spirit, whom Jesus has shared with us.

There is an advantage, though, to the repetition of the same phrase, whatever it is. It is a place to come back to from distractions; the rhythm disconnects the discursive mind and releases the deeper faculties.

65

The purpose of this meditation is not to accumulate a whole rosary of insights but rather to establish a conscious contact through Jesus Christ to our common Father. Once you have achieved that, merely rest in that awareness. At that point the words can fall away into a silent sharing of aliveness with God.

Creating Courage

Perhaps the greatest obstacle to people's continuing to pray is false expectations about what prayer is supposed to do and the principal misapprehension is that its purpose is somehow to change God's mind.

"Oh, God, please make me less weak, less prone to temptation!" Or, "Oh, God, don't let my mother die!" Or, "Oh, God, please end this war!" All of these begin to sound like attempts to remind a God who has grown absent-minded in old age that we are in need of help.

Sometimes such prayers of pleading even seem to presuppose a hard-hearted puppet master manipulating every event in our lives, and we poor wretches come crawling to this sadist trying to make him more loving.

People who complain that their prayers are never answered seem to forget that "No" is, in fact, an answer.

For whatever their reasons, God did create a universe in which evil was possible—both the physical evils of hurricanes and cancer, and the moral evils that result from human misuse of freedom. But our pitiable attempts to demand reasons for such a universe, from a God who is unanswerable to us, very subtly betray our ignorance or our unwillingness to accept "the way things are" which *is* the will of God. These attempts treat God almost as an equal—who just happens to have more power, like a very rich and famous uncle called by a poor relative into court where both stand as equals at the same bench. Job found how wrong that was.

A little quiet thought shows the glaring weakness in that demand. It is not unlike the innocent arrogance of earlier men and women who thought that, because we are on it, all the planets must revolve around the earth. Hard as the idea may be to accept, we are not the center of the universe, nor are we the center of reality.

Prayers of petition are not as reprehensible as I may have made them sound. There are times when we helplessly plead, "Just make it stop!" Moses prayed his soldiers might win battles. Martha prayed Jesus would bring her brother back. And in the Garden of Gethsemane, the Best of us begged his Father to take the chalice of suffering away.

The difference, I think, between us and Moses and Martha is that these people knew what they were doing. They didn't expect or demand that things be changed. Their prayers were more like the outpourings of one friend to another friend who was no more capable of changing things than they themselves. When a friend pours out her sorrows, she is not expecting her friend to bring back the dead. She is merely drawing some sustenance and strength from sharing her sorrow with someone who understands and loves and supports her with his presence.

Our Lady knew how to do it. At the wedding feast at Cana, she didn't say, "All right, now. What are you going to do about the wine situation?" Much less, "After all the things I've done for you, young man, you could at least...." No. All she said was, "They have no wine." And she left it to Jesus to do what he thought fit.

God did create someone to be an answer to your prayers: you. Prayers like, "Oh, God, help me pass this exam," and "Oh, God, help me stop losing patience with the kids," depend far more for their fulfillment on the person praying than on God. And they have far more likelihood of coming true if the prayer realizes where the responsibility for their fulfillment truly lies. The supplicant has just come to a Friend to be *reminded* of what has to be done.

Other petitionary prayers like "God, cure my father's cancer" are requests for things out of our hands and, in most cases, the result of the natural order of things, in which even God needn't be the principal influence at the moment. Such prayers are less frustrating when we understand that here, too, we are merely asking for courage to endure the results of the situation, should they turn out to be painful.

I think it is even worth picking our words carefully when we make such prayers of petition, so we actually do recognize that we are really asking not for a miracle but for the support of a Friend, the awareness of God's presence as we ourselves try to understand and cope and for the ability to see this event not from our cramped this-world point of view but from God's point of view. In the face of an eternity of celebration—as God sees it—this time of pain is as brief as the wake of a ship.

As Louis Evely says, when we make a petitionary prayer for someone else, the effect of that prayer should be that we do something for that person ourselves: write a letter, send a book, give a visible sign, a mini-sacrament. Such prayers are reminders not to God but to oneself. As C. S. Lewis wrote, it is far easier to pray for a boor than to visit him. When we ask God to take care of our spouses or parents or children, it should be a suggestion to oneself: "I've got to find a way to surprise them."

The best teachers render themselves unnecessary. The same is true of God. God is best served when his children realize that they must assume the role of their brother Jesus in changing the world. It will be gradual, imperfect, not a world where miracles are commonplace—unless we ourselves, adult sons and daughters of God, become the miracle workers.

Be careful what you ask of God. You are really asking it of yourself—and asking God to back you up while you do it. If you pray for the end of whatever war is currently in the news, you are really asking yourself to write a letter to the appropriate lawmaker or government body.

Prayer is not a practical thing, in the sense that it is not an attempt to get things done as a direct result of the prayer, to change things outside oneself—including God's mind. It is, rather, an attempt to change things *inside* oneself: the weakness, the cowardice, the irritation or even rage at "the way things are," the inertia that keeps us from helping those in need or crying out against vincible stupidity and injustice.

The reason we pray is to realize, once again, that we are not alone, that we have the greatest of Friends always beside us—not to do our jobs for us, as a weaker father might, but to support our courage to do our jobs for ourselves.

Prayer is, quite simply, presence and companionship. Just as all acts of love are.

EXERCISE

Step 1. Go very calmly through the relaxation exercises, un-tensing your body, slowing down your breathing, putting your consciousness into a state of receptive peace. Verge into the presence of God.

Step 2. Very, very slowly meditate on each phrase of the Our Father—even pausing and poring over it word by word. For instance, why is it "our" and not "my"? Aren't both true? What does it mean in the depth of myself? And so on. There is no need to move on to the next word or phrase until the present one has temporarily exhausted itself for you. No need to hurry. You don't have to get through the whole prayer. If you don't even get past the first word or two, it will have been a truly fine prayer.

The purpose of this exercise is also to consider, in each phrase, what you are really asking of this God of light and air and aliveness—and what you are asking of yourself.

Finding Intimacy With God

Another obstacle to continued praying is one's fear that it is ineffectual—not in the sense of changing God's mind but in the sense of your not "getting anything out of it." In the first place, achieving an ease at prayer takes time. But we've been conditioned by the rush of the competitive world, the expectations of others. We feel guilty unless we "ransom the time," come up with some concrete proof that we've really been working. Also, we are perhaps conditioned more than we suspect by advertisements leading us to expect unconditional, money-back guarantees for anything on which we have expended time or effort.

Many people, especially beginners, think the ten or fifteen minutes have been somehow wasted if they don't come out the other end with some great new insight or some brilliant new rephrasing of an old insight or something to share verbally with others. This is one reason I dislike the idea of keeping some kind of "prayer journal"—unless of course a particular individual finds it actually helpful.

Such journal logging, in the first place, turns what should be a deepening realization of presence and companionship into something like a diet regimen, with the dieter always checking petty advances and petty failures. But what's more important, we do not subject our meetings with other friends to such appraisal: "Did that work? Are we better friends than we were last time? Did I make any mistakes or progress?" Then why do it with our attempts to know

God better? It turns prayer into a Dale Carnegie class, with God as the potential customer.

By allowing the fear of being ineffectual to enter into the state of prayer and by wishing to accomplish something, we spoil it all. It shows that I want to be in charge, I want to see results, and I want to see them damn quick, d'ya hear? Then God is not at the center of the prayer; I am.

That reminds me of the cleaning lady who came into my room one day. She usually finds me typing away as furious as a piston on my computer. That day, she found me just sitting there, staring into space, daydreaming, thinking. And she said, "Oh, you're not working today. That's nice." Her comment meant to me that unless there is a noise and dancing fingers, unless there is a tangible product, you are really not thought to be doing anything.

Such a beneath-the-surface Puritanism used to infect me on retreats. Over the course of eight days of sequential meditations in *The Spiritual Exercises*, one expects recognizable progress: first, sin and repentance; second, the life of Christ; third, the Passion; fourth, the Resurrection and the meditation on love.

But one of the best retreats I ever made—and I have made over forty of them (two for thirty days each)—I went all alone to a cottage at a lake, and I said, "I'm not going to make any progress. I'm not going to start on Meditation #1 and move inexorably to Meditation #2. I'm just going to spend eight days 'hangin' out with Jesus, like two spouses with a week away from the kids."

And for a week, the two of us did just that: took long walks together, talked a bit—mostly, of course, about me—but a large part of the time the two of us sat silently together, just watching the water and the trees and the sky. It wasn't the least bit "useful." I didn't "learn" anything I didn't know before. But it was peaceful, and it was time well spent alone with a Friend. I've made every retreat since then like that.

Prayer is not a time to seek ready-made answers; sometimes they do actually come, seemingly out of nowhere, but they can't be predicted, or expected, much less demanded. What I seek is not answers but one particular realization: a very real contact with the deepest part of myself and a merging of that deepest self into the rhythm, the light, and the life of the living God, dwelling within me and all around me.

Come to prayer with no expectations. Be empty and expectant before God. It is not up to you to manufacture the light; all you have to do is open your self-protective shutters and raise the blinds. Those who approach prayer with only their intelligence seem almost to expect to "conquer God," like mastering the theory of relativity.

On the contrary, prayer is an opening of the self, making a place for God in your day and in your spirit, and inviting God into that opening. When you do that, you find God was already there, waiting to be noticed.

EXERCISE

Step 1. Begin with the relaxation, deep-breathing exercises outlined earlier. Remember that prayer need not be a matter of words, though there is nothing wrong with words. In your deepest concentration, plan the route for a ten- or fifteen-minute walk in a place where you know you will not be too disturbed. Pause for a minute before you begin and open yourself to God, acknowledge God's presence—with words like "Hello, there!" or "Hiya! I'm back again."

Step 2. Then just set off on your walk as you would with any other good friend. Tell God about your day as you would tell any friend who had gone through the day with you. "What did you think about…?" And then pause, give God a chance to answer. Most often you won't get a direct answer. Like the best of friends, God gets joy in just listening to you prattle on. As with any good friend, knowing God, you can probably guess what God would say anyway. But nonetheless still ask. Stop when you feel like it and look—really look—at the things you pass. If there's no need to speak of it, merely look, conscious that God is looking at it with you and through you.

I need say nothing of how to end it. Who am I to tell two friends how to end a walk together?

CHOOSING THE CONTEXT FOR PRAYER

Every year when I quiz my seminar groups about how they feel about prayer, the answers are varied but, almost without exception, the respondents say that they actually pray *sometimes*. Also, almost everyone says that they pray "sort of, when they need to." I would guess that this situation is true of most Christians who, outside of Mass—which is usually an uptight, mandated kind of prayer—pray only "when the spirit moves."

I wonder, though, if this is really the capital-S Spirit of God or the small-s spirit of human confusion and need. There is nothing wrong with praying from a desire to achieve some good or avoid some suffering, but when that is the *only* time when "the spirit moves me," there is a strong suspicion prayer means little more than panhandling.

God is not some doddering old miser who sits in his dark house, and who is worth a grudging visit just in case the old fool will be willing to fork over

76

this time. Nor does God sit there nursing hurt feelings because "The only time you visit me is when you want a handout." Hard as it is to admit, God doesn't need us—either our praise or our petitions or our thanksgiving. The point is that we need God, if we are to achieve the fullness of personhood of which we are capable. And we ought not waste time worrying about God's hurt feelings at being ignored but rather about what happens inside ourselves when we treat the Author of our lives as nothing more than a rare shoulder to cry on or an easy touch for a loan.

There are certain things in everybody's life that are considered essentials: eating, sleeping, being with people, taking a shower. We all have to do those things, and we usually not only find time for them each day but do them at about the same time of the day.

There are also things we get done even when we feel down and out: feeding the baby, emptying the garbage, taking a tray up to someone sicker than we. If prayer is truly an essential part of our lives, not just a temporary fad, not just a time killer like television soap operas, then it seems it should have a place set aside for it in our day, and we should make the small but definite decision about when it will be.

And prayer truly is essential for us, not only as humans but as Christians. As human beings we need time to regain our inner stability, time to re-collect the self—not the vague and surface "I" of everyday life but the real "I." The solitude that prayer demands lets us face our true selves without all the posturing and pretense that helps us bluff our way through the day. When one is alone, he or she is not necessarily a better person, but he or she is surely more genuine.

As Christians, too, we need prayer. Without a real contact with the Person about whom the theology texts were written and whom the Mass celebrates, we are dealing with nothing more involving than the philosophical system of a dead rabbi and attending a meeting no more religious than a Kiwanis luncheon for a Guest of honor who never shows up. One cannot remain a Christian for very long without praying.

Without it, we are no more than pagans with Christian labels.

Finding a Time for Prayer

The people for whom prayer is a kind of accident turn to it only when they find themselves alone and in need. But there is a great difference between finding yourself alone and *putting* yourself alone, in order to recognize your need for contact with the aliveness of God. As Jesus himself said, "When you pray, go into your room and close the door behind you."

There is no single answer to the question, "What time of day should I pray?" In a sense, there are as many answers to that question as there are people who pray.

Some find prayer easier in the morning when they are fresh; others can't really get all their circuits working until midmorning. Many find it easiest to pray at night when things have quieted down; others are just too bushed to focus their consciousness on anything more demanding than late-night television shows.

Each person has to find the best time for prayer and, among the times open in the day, must experiment to discover which of those free times he or she finds fruitful, which time is easiest in which to relax attentively, which time in which it is easier to make quiet contact with God.

There are certain areas of "fat" in anyone's day: riding to work or school, waiting outside offices, stalled in traffic. Surely one of those unavoidable waits can be used to pray rather than merely read the newspaper. Surely we could spare fifteen minutes out of our time for passive relaxations—which we truly need but perhaps not for as long as we let them stretch on.

We are humans and inventive, so it is possible for us to find creative nooks in our schedules for the process of prayer. One young student told me he always prayed in the bathroom every morning and, to be sure, it is a time alone none of us can avoid!

It is not at all important *when* we take the time to pray. The real point is *that* we take the time—and on a regular basis.

Finding a Place for Prayer

The particular place chosen for prayer is not important either, although most people who achieve an ease with meditation find it good to have one kind of "base" where they can be sure of some solitude and silence for a while. In a way, the ability to find some place like that will be a factor in what time of the day one chooses to meditate—when everyone is out of the house, when you have the office to yourself, when the park isn't clamorous with kids and dogs. A great many people have no privacy where they live or work and therefore have to find their seclusion outside their familiar world, in a chapel, on a park bench, along a path in the woods. But surely each of us can find some "secret place."

For many years I avoided praying in chapels because always, at the back of my tangled mind, I would wonder if other people were coming in behind me, seeing me, saying to themselves, "How wonderfully pious he is!" In the first place, I didn't want to be considered pious, and in the second place I kept foolishly debating with myself whether I was in a chapel only *because I* wanted to be seen and judged "good."

Such self-conscious idiocy was sure proof my prayer at those times was not a letting go, not an opening up to God, but a focusing on myself—and only the surface of that self at that. For those fifteen minutes, who cares who sees you or what they think! If a chapel is the only place in which you can find solitude and quiet in your world, use it. Presumably the other visitors are not there to keep watch on you. They are there for the same purpose you are: to be alone with God.

Preparing the Body for Prayer

The paradox about prayer is that the whole person has to be both relaxed and at the same time attentive. Our bodies are the major sources of distraction from achieving this quiet receptivity. They itch, they gurgle, they cramp, they tense up. They are lured out of concentration by the slightest sounds. The *Bhagavad-Gita,* the Hindu scriptures, say stillness of the mind in meditation should be like a candle flame in a windless place. But we live in a world where drafts come from the most unexpected places. As a result, many modern books on prayer give a great deal of attention to methods of body control in order to lessen distractions and focus the attention of those who meditate.

As with choosing a time and place, choosing a position most conducive to prayer is a matter of individual experiment. Even within a single prayer period, the position may alter as the body either gets in the way of concentration or, in more experienced meditators, moves naturally into a position which embodies the mood of the prayer. For instance, when someone is praying and begins to feel a sense of profound awe at the presence of God, he or she may move from a sitting position to kneeling position, even with the forehead to the floor.

To Westerners who are painfully uptight about body movements (except at rock concerts), the infinite ways the body can express inner spiritual states and even enhance them is severely limited. But if you are alone in your room, why worry who "sees" you?

In general, however, you should find a "rest" position in which you begin your prayer and remain there, even if it takes a kind of quiet self-discipline.

(In Zen prayer halls, there is a monk with a willowy stick who comes along and gives you a good sharp thwack if you become fidgety!)

The urge to get up and walk around is often a sign that the person is getting itchy, that the prayer is not being "effectual," that nothing is "happening." Controlling the urge to get up and move about very often is the threshold of a real inner breakthrough. Therefore, without making a big deal about bodily posture, it is worthwhile to find one or two basic "rest" positions that help you personally and stick with them, especially at the beginning.

Kneeling is the most traditional and obvious Western posture in prayer but, as many a religious novice can testify, kneeling can be a distraction in itself, focusing all one's attention not on the God who dwells within us but on the aching knees. If it helps symbolize your inner feelings at the time, kneel; if not, there are many other prayerful positions.

Lying flat on one's back is probably the most restful posture for prayer, but this position has one drawback: you often fall asleep.

Sitting is perhaps the best position in which to pray for most people. One can relax but at the same time be attentive and focused. Simply sit in a straight chair, head tilted slightly forward or backward, hands resting on the lap or the knees.

The masters of Zen are convinced that the sitting posture known as the lotus position is the best posture for prayer. They believe that somehow this position "organizes" the whole body—breathing, movement of the blood, even the composition of body fluids—to such an extent that the whole body is under control, nonintrusive, at peace. In the full lotus, one sits on the edge of a pillow or step, knees widespread, feet crossed at the calves and each foot resting on the crook of the opposite knee. (That's the hard part!) The hands rest on the heels, fingers resting on one another, thumbs slightly touching to make the hands a little circle.

In his book *Christian Zen,* William Johnston says:

> *The lotus position somehow impedes discursive reasoning and thinking; it somehow checks the stream of consciousness that flows across the surface of the mind; it detaches one from the very process of thinking. Probably it is the worst position for philosophizing but the best for going down to the center of one's being in imageless and silent contemplation.*

A great difficulty about the lotus position is that Westerners, not used to sitting without support, find at least the full lotus difficult to sustain and as distracting as kneeling. A variation of this position, the half-lotus, is little different from sitting cross-legged, "Indian style." For those unable to endure the full lotus, sit with your back relatively straight, comfortable yet not comfortable enough to fall asleep.

The important thing about posture for prayer is that it should be comfortable enough to eliminate distractions but not so comfortable as lounging.

Prayer should be a time when you are at ease but not so at ease as to be "all over the place." Sprawling destroys the concentration of your full consciousness.

Control of breathing can be very helpful in putting the body at the service of the soul. Every prayer period should begin with some conscious exercise to withdraw yourself from the daily fuss and rush, to focus on the person—your self—whom you are offering to unite with the divine presence within you. One way of getting "into" yourself is to focus on your breathing.

It takes more than a little practice to be able to sit and meditate, as Zen initiates do, with the eyes open. I personally still cannot do it except at very special times, such as near water or by a fire or below a sky ablaze with stars. In a way, the eyes are the hungriest of our senses, and they insist on darting about, taking everything in. This curiosity is admirable most of the time, but when you are trying to focus all your powers *inside* yourself, the eyes can be a powerful distraction. Even Buddhists who can meditate open-eyed usually focus their eyes on a crack in the floor or a spot on the wall and lock them there until the spot has no new evidence, no unexplored aspect to lead the mind away.

Another way I find helpful to pray open-eyed is to focus on a small space where the sun lances through the thick leaves of a tree and in my imagination picture it as God "leaking through" the surfaces of everything it enlivens.

Another means Eastern adepts use to ensure an undistracted posture for prayer is the mandala, some physical object with symbolic value that focuses the attention. They realize that once the eyes begin to wander they are lost. Some Christians use a crucifix as a mandala, holding it lightly in their laps and focusing *into* it and what it means.

In most modern churches, for liturgical reasons, to make the altar the center of attention, the tabernacle with its flickering red lamp has been moved to one side. This is fine, I suppose, for the majority of Christians whose only prayer time is an hour on Sunday, but a regrettable loss of one more mandala for the smaller number of Christians who like to drop into a church and pray more than once a week.

Enlisting a Director for Prayer

Beginners serious about prayer who want to pray by choice and not by chance really should seek some wise man or woman to advise them about prayer. The most obvious advantage is having the chance to talk unabashedly about praying to someone who not only understands its importance to you but who also prays. It's nice to know you're not the only one trying!

Having a director is also a source of new ideas, new ways to relax and focus your consciousness. Talking every few weeks to a fellow pray-er seems, at least to me, a far better prayer strategy than keeping a "prayer journal"; and an advisor can not only keep you at it but can also give you a kick in the pants when you are being overly pious or overly serious about yourself.

If praying makes you an old stick-in-the-mud, you're surely doing something wrong. When prayer is true and honest and really in touch with the aliveness of God, it should not be cramping but liberating. The people I know who pray the best seem able to spread a quiet joy wherever they go. And why not? The aliveness of God should be the most joyful infection around!

SOME METHODS
OF PRAYING

No matter what our age, sex, or color, all human beings have needs and hopes and vices in common. At the same time, though, no two of us has precisely the same tastes and susceptibilities. Therefore, in a book like this, it is impossible to suggest the one sure-fire method of praying suitable for everybody. Therefore, I offer the few methods I know in the hopes one or two may prove useful.

Also, some methods work well for a while, then start to wither away. It is helpful to have others to fall back on when one method ceases to be fruitful.

Genuine prayer always has some constants, though: the deliberate withdrawal into solitude, the active attempt to focus your consciousness, and the awareness of the Other. Without that "connection," you are just sitting there brooding. But the methods, the content, the communication itself will vary from person to person, from occasion to occasion.

The Mantra

Transcendental meditation has adapted some of the methods of Eastern mysticism, not necessarily to help people pray but merely, on the human level, to assist meditators in the achievement of some peace and to marshal their consciousness to live and work more effectively and with a greater sense of fulfillment.

After exercises in relaxation, regulating breathing, and concentrating consciousness, the student of transcendental meditation receives a mantra, usually in Sanskrit. The meditator is completely ignorant of the meaning of the Sanskrit word or phrase. The meaning of the words is not as important as the rhythms, the way the constant and peaceful repetition of the sound limits the rational consciousness to *one* process: achieving a kind of "one-pointedness." In so doing, it opens up the unused power of the mind and spirit into an area of the self ordinarily dormant.

Mantras are a fairly simple form of achieving peace. They are also a good guard against distraction—like the tangible mandala—and something to return to if the attention wanders off. The sheer boredom that the repetition induces in the logical mind forces the consciousness downward—like the hypnotic effect of watching flames or listening to the drumming of the rain or the harrumph of the waves. It almost inevitably makes one meditative.

The most famous mantra is "OM," which the subject repeats over and over, feeling the vibrations thrumming resonantly in the chest, yielding to the sound and vibrations. "The Jesus Prayer" mentioned in a previous exercise is also a kind of mantra.

When done rightly, so is the rosary—which is not only a Christian practice but a Buddhist one as well. It doesn't matter that you don't grasp the words of the Our Fathers and Hail Marys. As a matter of fact, you *shouldn't*. The repetitiveness of the words is *supposed* to disconnect you from thinking. Just as with most of our lunchtime conversations (which are not worth recording to ponder later), there are *two* "conversations" going on: one is the surface chit-chat, the other more important one is saying "I enjoy being with you." The same is true conversing with God.

EXERCISE

Begin with the usual relaxation and deep-breathing exercises.

Step 1. After quieting the senses, repeat a single word—"Jesus" or "Father" or "love"—very quietly and calmly over and over and over, feeling the vibrations and rhythms, losing yourself in the words and the realities that they embody. (When I am distracted, the word "OM" does it every time. It even distracts me from motion sickness on an airplane!)

Step 2. As an alternative or extension to the previous step, you may wish to tape record your mantra or use a recording of mantralike music, such as Gregorian chant, as a means of meditating your consciousness into a prayer state.

90 The Koan

Many poems and many parts of Scripture are so cryptic that we read them once, presume they are "meaningless for me," and pass on. We have been conditioned by the easy-access Pablum of television to expect that anything worth hearing or reading will of course be in words any backward three-year-old could understand. We have also been conditioned by our education to expect that a teacher will explain anything murky *for* us so that we need never figure out anything for ourselves and disconnect ourselves from our intelligence. Thus, we impoverish ourselves.

Eastern mystics, however, have taken precisely the opposite tack. One of their methods is the koan, a seemingly unanswerable riddle which the Zen master gives a student. The master tells the student to pore over the riddle hour after hour. The most famous koan is: "We know the sound of two hands clapping. What is the sound of one hand clapping?"

Oddly, the focusing of the consciousness, the intensity of quiet concentration, the prolonged dedication, suddenly causes the persistent monk to burst through into enlightenment. Basically, the koan is a gimmick to frustrate the mind at its upper level of discursive, rationalizing logic and thus force it to break through, down into a deeper level of psychic activity.

EXERCISE

Begin with the usual preparatory, deep-breathing exercises. Make sure that your breathing is calm and even and that you have centered yourself in readiness for prayer.

Step 1. After finding your focus, engage your attention with one of the many seemingly impossible statements of the Scriptures:

- "The innocent suffer while the wicked prosper."

- "Sell all you have, give to the poor, and come follow me."

- "This is my Body."

- "If you want the first place, take the last place."

- "I live now—not I, but Christ lives in me."

Step 2. Approach the koan by beginning with a mantra, such as "Jesus" or "my Father," and establish a kind of bass rhythm to your prayer. Then, with the basic rhythm regularized by means of your breathing, turn your attention to the statement of the koan and ponder it, weigh it, roll it around in your mind against the rhythmic background of the mantra. This method may sound foolish, but it works!

Remember: you are not trying to figure out these scriptural koans logically, like a riddle or a math problem. These one-sentence, apparently impossible statements from Scripture are—like our physical, surface bodies—only the tip of the iceberg. For instance, when someone you have loved for a long time suddenly says, "You know what? I really love you," there is a whole universe of meaning behind those words. Compared to the host of meanings they contain, the words and sounds that carry the meanings are as thin and unsubstantial as husks.

And when you sit and ponder those words—"I love you"—echoing in the back of your mind in the voice of someone you love, you do not list the meanings or count them or sort them out logically. You immerse yourself in them, moving intuitively and joyfully from one into the other and back again. And while you are reveling in those unnumbered beautiful meanings, there is no awareness of time or place or distractions.

Try hearing God say the same thing to you. "I…really…love…you."

Hard to believe, huh? Yet, impossibly, it's true.

Scripture: Pondering Ideas

Many people are turned off by the Scriptures because they seem so impenetrable. Often this response
is caused by taking too much in one bite. Other times
we are hampered by doubts. "Was there really a star
to guide the Magi?" Or by stupid questions, "Did
Adam have a navel?" Or by using Scripture to prove
or attack the claims of Christianity, "If Jesus actually
walked on water, how come...?"

Forget all the complications and let the words enter your guts where they can begin to live. As William Johnston says, "Let them live....Get the kick those
Semitic writers are trying to give you. Then you'll
find the Scriptures are food and that they are life."

EXERCISE

Begin your prayer session with the deep-breathing, relaxation exercise as usual. Have a copy of the
Scriptures handy—preferably a copy that provides
positive sensory feedback in terms of paper, read-
able type, and so forth.

Step 1. Sit with the Scriptures in your lap. Relax,
pull away from the world, and center your consciousness on the inner powers deep inside of you.

Then open the Scriptures any place and begin
to focus that inner power on God's elusive communication through the words on the page. (If you

happen to open to the genealogy of Jesus, or some such similar passage, move along until you find a passage that engages your interest in a deeper way!) Just be sure to make the section small, no more than four or five verses. Some people like to start, say, at the beginning of an epistle and move gradually, day by day, through it.

Step 2. Whether you open at random or work steadily from part to part, the important thing is to take small bites. Rest in each small bite, savor them as you did the koan. "What are these strange words trying to say to me?" There is no need at all to "get through" or "knock off" another epistle or gospel. Just proceed at your own pace.

If you are unfamiliar with Scripture and are uncomfortable with a random walk through its pages, you may wish to try these passages:

- Isaiah 6:6-8
- Matthew 25:37-40
- Mark 8:31-33
- Luke 14:12-14
- John 1:1-5, 9-14

- Romans 7:4-6
- 1 Corinthians 12:8-13
- Ephesians 3:14-19
- Philippians 2:5-11
- Hebrews 5:1-4

If it helps, picture yourself as a prophet or evangelist or epistle writer who feels the inner stirrings of this message from God for the very first time. "And the word of God came to me saying...." What does it mean? Why is God saying it to *me*?

Controlled Daydreaming

There is a difference between mulling over the ideas of Scripture and reliving Scripture in your imagination. Ideas still have some relationship to the discursive intelligence and, because most of us are more used to working on that level, I treated ideas first: the kinds of mental activities one associates with school essays, discussions, lectures, probing ideas from different angles, even trying to logic-chop poems for meaning. And indeed there is much in Scripture that concerns itself with handling truth in that mode.

But Scripture is not only a repository of ideas about life which Jesus offered. Scripture is also a story about a Person. Not only were the words he spoke a revelation of Good News but his actions were also revelatory. Therefore, one can not only mull over his ideas but also can learn from trying in the imagination to relive the gospel story. However, we are much more conditioned by our education to discuss and debate ideas than to relive a story within the framework of our imaginations.

When I was a kid, long before anyone dreamed of television, I used to lie on the floor for an hour every evening listening to our old Sonora radio spew out the adventures of Captain Midnight, Jack Armstrong, the Shadow, and the Green Hornet. These radio programs were real to me, alive. These adventures were not just produced by men and women standing in street clothes at microphones in some faraway stu-

95

dio. What I heard was really an on-the-spot broad-cast from the headwaters of the Orinoco, and Jack and Billy and Betty were exuding sweat as they squat-ted in real muck to escape the vicious Auca Indians. My imagination took those sounds and built a world out of them, sometimes more real than the radio it-self and the carpet I was sprawled on.

As I think about it, it must have been easier to re-create new worlds with one's imagination in the cold stone dining halls of medieval castles as a minstrel spun out the tales of Arthur and Beowulf for the en-raptured. It must have been easier to visualize the story of the gospels in the dank darkness of the cata-combs. For most of the world's history, words alone were enough for strong imaginations to summon up the actual places and persons in any story.

Today, however, most of our visualization is done for us. We needn't imagine Mr. Spock's pointy ears as the Klingons creep toward him across the rocks of some unpronounceable planet. The picture is right there. The only job the imagination has is to lull us into a state of suspended disbelief that these are merely impulses on the flat surface of a cathode ray tube.

Children, by the way, still have some vestige of real-ization left; some of them wonder when Mommy is going to dust up all those dead bad guys from the floor of the television set. But they get over that quickly.

It was probably easier to pray, too, in the days before the mass media assumed our powers of thinking and visualizing for us. Not only were there fewer distractions then, and fewer passive entertainments with which to wile away the empty hours, but the very lack of prefab images made the individual's imagination work far more, strengthen itself, reach.

An audience looking at Shakespeare's nearly barren stage could visualize its own bushes and trees and starry, spangled skies—with little more than Shakespeare's poetry to evoke it from the rich wells of their own sense memories, far more sensitized than ours.

The person who brings a well-stocked and sensitive imagination to prayer has a great deal more going for him or her than one who has let visualization become passive. We are, after all, trying to contact a way of existing and a Person who can never be adequately concretized.

The God we pray to appears with numberless facets—love, anger, mercy, justice; God made a world out of nothing and turned death into a doorway. To cope with such a mercurial Being takes a person capable of keeping all sorts of colored balls spinning in the air at once. We are all, in a sense, *les jongleurs de Dieu* when we pray.

It seems wise, therefore, to offer a few limbering up exercises for those who feel their imaginations have sagged and are unable to tap the rich source of energy lurking below the surface mind, a source of creative power that can make the Scriptures come alive and realized.

EXERCISE

Do a preliminary relaxation and deep-breathing exercise to clear the sense of stimuli actually working on you at the moment. Let your mind become a clear, clean slate.

Step 1. The purpose of this step is to focus all your powers on re-creating the sense-memory of the object designated in the exercise. In the case of each sense, the objects become more and more subtle, and therefore more and more difficult to re-create, to real-ize.

Taste: Try to re-create in your memory and imagination the taste of garlic, the smell of it on your fingers when you dice it. Feel what it does to your tongue, the roof of your mouth, your throat, your nose. Don't move on to the next taste object until you have "got" garlic. Then try a particular flavor of chewing gum, spearmint, for example. Again, be sure you have the taste before going on. Then, re-create the taste of a chocolate bar. Since all the senses work together, include in the taste the sound of the wrapper ripping, the texture and sound of the foil, the movement of your teeth and tongue as you chew. Next, sense the taste of strawberry ice cream. Then, the difference between margarine and butter.

Texture: Re-create the feel of the rough bark of a tree… burlap…nylon…a pile of dry leaves… pudding…sand between your toes…skin…hair. Again, you feel not only with your hands but with your cheeks and your feet. Make the re-creation as real as you can.

Movement: Here, too, feel the sensations not only in your eyes as an observer but actually in movements which affect your own body: in your hands and all your muscles, your back, your legs, the blood in your head. Re-create the movement of jumping on a trampoline…rowing a small boat in choppy waters…walking in knee-deep water by a lake or along a creek…running on wet pavement…leaping off the high diving board…standing at attention in the hot sun.

Sound: Reexperience the moment not only with your ears but with the reactions that the sounds set up in the pit of your stomach, on the hairs at the back of your neck: a crack of thunder at night and its receding rumblings…crackling flames at a fire in the woods…water poured on the ashes of the fire…a single pair of footsteps on a dark street… an empty office late at night…a dripping faucet.

Sight: A flash of lightning on a steamy afternoon…sunset over water or behind hills or buildings (they're quite different)…catsup on a greasy burger…the oily surface of a cup of tepid coffee

…sunlight on a window sill…"a red wheelbarrow glazed with rain beside the white chickens."

Step 2. Now try to focus all your sense-memories of a single object of food—a piece of plain white bread, a stalk of crisp green celery, a peppermint candy. Choose just one. In your imagination, pick it up, feel its textures, bring it right up to your nose and sniff its fragrance. Put it in your mouth and feel the muscles working, hear the sound they make working together. Then try to sum up the whole experience as if it were happening right now.

Step 3. Now use all the senses, step by step, on a scene—a stormy night alone in a hilltop cabin, riding in a car late at night, a hot afternoon at the beach, your first date. Let your imagination move from object to object, moment to moment, as if you were right there.

Even though you have never been to such a place at such a time, your imagination can take you there. Stored up in your sense-memories are all the tastes, smells, colors, sounds, and movements of your past, and from them you can fabricate a situation you have never actually experienced.

Obviously these exercises couldn't be called prayer, although they could lead to it. They truly are an attempt to pull out of the rat race in which we rush heedlessly past most of the objects of God's creation.

Scripture: Inner Visualization

One of the reasons so few people enjoy reading literature—especially plays—is that they have not trained themselves to visualize what is actually going on. The same is true of reading Scripture. Our minds are so clotted with the witless attempts Hollywood has made at embodying the stories and also with the cloying plaster statues that clutter our churches, schools, and dashboards that we rarely make the effort to visualize for ourselves our own Jesus, Mary, Nicodemus, Judas.

More than one meditation time could concentrate on conjuring up what Jesus really looked like, as if *you* were casting a movie: his flesh color, his hair, his face, his body. Don't settle on the plastic stereotype of the blue-eyed, long-haired, white-robed image. If it helps, look at copies of *National Geographic* for pictures of young Israeli men who have spent a great deal of time outdoors. Another approach: how would Jesus look today? What kind of clothes would he wear? Use all your senses to "capture" Jesus.

What we are looking for is an inner visualization, using all your sense memories of sight, touch, taste, hearing, and smell to re-create for yourself an event of the gospels. Feel free in the scene, be part of it—either as one of the participants or as some anonymous passerby. Run your hands over the rough textures of the animals at the Nativity. Feel your nose and throat and toes clotted with the dust as Jesus walks along the roads with his friends. Hear the clang of the hammers and the jeers of the crowds on the hill of Calvary. Smell the sweat. Just pick the event—any event in the gospels—and *be* there.

One method of doing this I stumbled on during a retreat. I was having a dry time of it, four or five hourlong meditations each day, and when I came to the episode of Jesus washing his disciples' feet, I hit a dead standstill. I couldn't visualize it at all; I couldn't even get started. They were all the pasteboard stereotypes of the cheap holy cards, not human beings.

My wise spiritual director, knowing that such times are the sign one is getting close to a breakthrough, said merely, "Okay, do it again." I ground my teeth but I tried.

This time, however, instead of trying to visualize the scene out of thin air, I decided I'd conjure up not the apostles sitting around the Last Supper table but the Jesuits of my own community. And instead of "becoming" just one of the disciples (as I had always with false humility done), I took the place of Jesus—since after all, he'd said, "Just as I'm washing your feet, you must wash one another's feet."

Suddenly that scene had a whole new reality and meaning! I'd look up at the imagined face of each member of my community and say, "Of course. It's a privilege to wash your feet…and yours." But then at the next, I stopped: "I'll be *damned* if I'll wash your feet, you self-centered drone!" What an insight.

EXERCISE

Begin by setting your breathing at a rhythmic pace. Clear your mind and enter a receptive, calm place.

Step 1. Choose any event in the Scriptures that has special resonance for you. Read the passage slowly. Then put the book aside. Begin at the very beginning and be there, sense-memories alive and probing, and move step by step with people you know.

Step 2. One of the most readily accessible scenes to re-create is the Passion. Put yourself in Jesus' place. Feel the wood on your shoulders, spittle running down your cheek, the raw flesh on your back, the blows, the crush of bodies. Smell the sweat, the stinking breath, the sour wine, the dust. Step by step. The next time you see a crucifix it will look different.

PRAYING WHEN YOU DON'T FEEL LIKE IT

Few people run around all day mumbling the name of Jesus. A thousand events clutter our waking hours, demand time, energy, attention. Very honestly, at times—even if we have a deep conviction that praying is important—the spirit may be willing but the flesh just digs in its heels. You can plunk yourself down into a perfect lotus position and grit your teeth as you face an intimidatingly blank wall, and the spirit joins the flesh in seething restlessness. That's the time to realize no one can achieve peace and contact with the deep self every day of the year.

But it needn't be a day without some kind of prayer; it's just a day for a different kind. There are far more possibilities than I outline here, but I offer them for a rainy day, some of them "doing" prayers, some remembering prayers—a more discursive kind of prayer than we have considered so far.

Rewriting Scripture

Meditating on Scripture, in the real sense, means merely letting the meaning of a short passage seep into you, as we have seen. But at moments when the old devil of progress demands some kind of visible results, some kind of physical movement, one way to thwart it is to compromise with your mood instead of forgoing prayer completely. Anyone who has rambled through the Scriptures has a favorite psalm or paragraph in the gospels that has always "talked" to him or her, even though it seems dull as dust this particular day.

A book by the chaplain of the Buffalo city jail gives the results of what young criminals did to the Scriptures. For instance, one boy took Psalm 23 ("The Lord is my shepherd…"). To a street-tough kid, the image of a gentle keeper of sheep is utterly without content. So this kid came up with, "The Lord is my probation officer…," using the best image he could find of a kindly and protective leader willing to sacrifice to keep a youngster out of further trouble.

More cautious people might think that this "translation" is disrespectful. But in the first place the Scriptures intend to communicate not just to literary purists but to all men, women, and children. That's what Jesus did. In the second place even Paul says the Spirit of Jesus within us enables us to call God "Abba"—not "Eminent Sir" or "Divine Parent." It doesn't even mean "Father." It meant "Papa." So much for purists.

Here is a prayer I did one doldrummy day on Psalm 8. It was enough to keep me going a couple of days in the spiritual desert. Now that I've written it out, I can go back at times and slowly, prayerfully use it again, because it is *my* psalm now as much as that of the original psalmist.

O GOD, MY GOD
How utterly your presence
    fills all the earth!
The stars sing your glory
    back and forth across the night sky.
You made the wide-eyed children and their
    wonder
        to be your great surprise
            for the learned
            for the sophisticated
            for the cynical.
When I look up at the vast heavens—
    the moon and the stars that you made
        with your fingers
    and set spinning endless ages of space and
        time ago—
I wonder at you.
What is humankind
    that you care so much for us,
    that in this steady and loyal universe
        you chose such persnickety folk
            as us?
You made us only a little less than yourself.
You have crowned us with glory and honor.

You took all your hands had made
and gave all those wonders into
our hands—
darkness and light,
waters and sky,
plants and trees and their seed,
the fish of the sea,
the birds of the air,
and all the beasts of the field,
because, of all your creatures,
only we are made in your image
and likeness.
Who are we, that you care so much for us?
O GOD, MY GOD!
How utterly your presence fills all the earth!

Here is one from the New Testament, an attempt to rewrite the first three beatitudes—to make them say something to me when the words I had been accustomed to didn't seem to yield anything any more:

How lucky you are when your spirit's
hungry; then you'll go out and find what will
fill it: the Kingdom of Heaven.

How lucky you are when you're in need of
comforting; then you'll realize how much
you need one another and our God.

How lucky you are when you're gentle and
willing to be taken in; then all the earth
opens up for you.

EXERCISE

Begin as usual with relaxation and deep-breathing exercises. Have patience with yourself and allow plenty of time to let your breathing take over for your muddled and recalcitrant mind.

Step 1. Get yourself a sheet of paper and a pen or pencil. Open your copy of the Scriptures to a passage that you like and start, line by line, to translate it into words and images that are meaningful to you. Try to imagine the Author of Scripture sitting beside you, interested, making suggestions, understanding very well that although you can't pray for a long stretch today, you are pondering his words and trying to assimilate them as well as you can at this moment.

Step 2. If the day is especially dreary and you are in need of more specific instructions, open to the gospel according to Matthew 5:3-12. Using the three examples I have given you, see what you can do with this passage along the same line. Remember, you don't have to finish all of the beatitudes. If you do one beatitude for the whole fifteen minutes, that's just fine and dandy!

Composing Prayers

When worse comes to worst, one way to pray when you want to but don't feel up to it is writing the prayer out. This technique is sort of like a short letter to God when God seems farther away than usual. It's a very honorable way to pray. After all, if the psalmists never wrote their prayers down, we'd never have had the psalms.

There is only one caution I would make about prayers one writes out. Most such prayers, once they're written, should be ripped up and thrown away. Otherwise, prayer could become something "useful," something with a physical product. Also, when the prayer is going to be filed someplace, one tends to begin fussing over pretty phraseology, when really the whole purpose of the prayer should be a spontaneous sharing of one's presence and aliveness, with no care about misplaced modifiers and spelling.

Some prayers you may want to keep, though. They are sometimes helpful when you are in the same kind of mood later on, triggering a more meditative kind of prayer all over again at a later date.

Here is one Augustine obviously decided was not only worth keeping but worth sharing:

> MY GOD
> *What is it that I love when I love you?*
> *Not the beauty of any bodily thing*
> *Nor the beauty of the seasons,*

Nor the brightness of light that rejoices
    the eye,
Nor the sweet melodies of all songs,
Nor the fragrance of flowers and
    ointments and spices,
Nor manna nor honey
Nor limbs that carnal love embraces.
None of these things do I love when I
    love my God.
Yet
in a sense
I do love light
    and melody
    and fragrance
    and food
    and embrace,
        when I love my God.
The light
and the voice
and the food
and the fragrance
and the embrace in the soul
    when the light shines upon my soul
        which no place can contain,
    when that voice sounds which no time
        can take away,
I breath a fragrance
    which no wind scatters;
I eat a food
    which is not lessened by the eating;
And I lie in an embrace

which satiety never comes to sunder.
This is what I love
    when I love my God.

112

In his novel, *Helena,* Evelyn Waugh composed this prayer and put it on the lips of the saintly mother of the Emperor Constantine. It is a prayer to the Magi—learned, rich men like the Empress herself—who seem to find small encouragement in a kingdom of God that shows such strong predilection for the poor and the unlettered.

Like me, you were late in coming.
For you the primordial discipline
    of the heavens was relaxed
    and a new defiant light blazed
    amid the disconcerted stars.
How laboriously you came
    taking sights and calculating.
How odd you looked on the road
    laden with such preposterous gifts.
Yet you came, and were not turned away.
Your gifts were not needed,
But they were accepted and put carefully by,
For they were brought with love.
Dear Cousins, pray for me,
    for His sake
    Who did not reject your curious gifts.
Pray always for all the learned
    the oblique,
    the delicate.

Let them not be quite forgotten
at the throne of God
when the simple come into their kingdom.

113

Finally, here is one I wrote myself, God knows when, which more or less sums up the mood one is in when he or she resorts to writing prayers rather than meditating:

DEAR GOD
I'm surrounded by "shoulds"
"When are you going to…?"
"You really ought to…."
"There's not much time left."
My desk is a disaster area.
Letters unanswered.
Assignments ungraded.
Unread books.
It makes a hollow fear in my belly
to realize
all the empty places still in my life,
all the promises I've made,
all the deadlines I've agreed to,
all that "they" expect of me,
all the things that,
because
I love them
and you
and my life,
I should do soon—
or sooner.

There is so much to do, and so little time.
They are all, each in its way, important.
But because you are the reason
    and the cause
    and the aliveness
        of all I have left to do,
Give me the wisdom to set aside this page
    and be with you.

114

In general, prayers such as this should be thrown away—in a sense, "sent," so that their purpose is to communicate with God, not to set up a stockpile of prayers for later reading. Except for the very best of them, written prayers should be just between my Friend and me.

EXERCISE

Begin as always by doing the preparatory deep-breathing, calming exercise. Envision your reluctance to spend time in prayer as a boat that will wash away on the tides.

Step 1. Find writing paper or stationery that suits your mood. You may wish to write on water-marked bond or on the backs of envelopes. Also select a writing instrument that encourages your thoughts—it may be a pencil stub, a fine-point pen, or crayons. First, decide on a salutation for this prayer-letter to God. Will it be "Dear God," "Dear Friend," or "To Whom It May Concern."

Step 2. Once these preparatory actions are taken, let your mind wander freely. Write what comes into your mind as if it were free-flowing into your fingertips and into your pen. Keep on writing for at least five minutes. Then pick an appropriate closing, for example, "Yours truly," "Love," or "See Ya Soon."

Remember that this exercise is merely a conduit to getting out of the doldrums—not an essay assignment. Once you are finished, tear up your letter and throw the pieces away.

Prayers for Walking, Waiting, Driving

This title could as well have been "Waiting Room Prayers" or "Driving the Car Prayers." There are times in the day when you are occupied-but-not-occupied: waiting for the dentist, scooting along the freeway, hustling along the sidewalk. There are distractions available with which to kill time: Musak, the shop window, the back-issue magazines at the chiropractor's office, idle scrutiny of passersby.

You could just as well use some of the time to find a little pocket of peace, to renew awareness of the divine aliveness you hold at the depths of your being. (This is not to say every spare moment has to be packed with prayer, only that it is one of the many things you are free to do. However, when prayer becomes a habit, you may find you are praying nearly all the time when you are alone. Because you are not alone.)

There are also times when you are too itchy to sit and meditate, times when there is not even the patience to sit and write prayers, times when you have to get the roof off your head. No problem. Just get out and start walking in the woods or in a park or even on a city street.

EXERCISE

Begin your "idle-time" prayer with a few deep breaths. Find one of your pulse points, feel the rhythm of your heartbeat, and pace your breathing accordingly.

Step 1. Close your eyes, if possible, and focus your consciousness on your Companion, and make "the connection." Find a mantra that will focus your attention. You may pick any key that will prime the pump for a snatch of prayer time, of "hangin' out with Jesus."

Step 2. When you are driving, walking, or waiting, focus your attention—one by one—on the people you love and who love you. This is not a quantitative struggle to fill up a mental photo album. This focus merely allows each one of those people to rise up into your consciousness, allows you to see their faces, ponder how much they mean to you, remember trials and joys you've shared, then thank God for allowing that person to exist and for steering the two of you together.

Don't rush on to the next person, like "God bless Mommy and Daddy and Uncle Fred and...." Let each person stay at the center of your attention, your one-pointedness, for as long as they will. Then let another take over. Savor them. Be grateful for them. And then that association will lead to another and another.

You can probably drive or walk for a full hour with those friends and wonder where the time has gone. But I am certain that when you get where you're going, you will have found joy. You will realize how fortunate you are, and there will be no difficulty thanking the Giver.

Autobiographical Prayer

Another method of "unstructured" prayer is to think back on the events and memories of your life, using these as springboards to prayerful meditation. We can use this self-reflection, not as a narcissistic endeavor, but as grateful reflection on our gifts.

EXERCISE

Begin with prayerful deep breathing. Find a center point where your heart is still and your mind cleansed.

Step 1. Think back to the first thing you can remember—a toy, a snowfall, a playmate—and move gradually through the years from event to event (not all of them pleasant), savoring, reassessing, expressing gratitude not only for the joyous moments but also for the painful ones which have made you wiser than you were before they occurred.

Step 2. If you are praying in the evening or late afternoon, you can do the same thing with your day, beginning from the first moment you awoke from your overnight stupor. Realize what a great moment that is—waking up to a new day—a gift we take so much for granted.

There is no rule that says you have to wake up every morning; there is a morning in the future when you won't wake up. So this morning was one more gift! Then move slowly through the events of the day, not like some "examination of conscience" but more as an examination of *consciousness*.

There will be regrets; fine, you've realized it at least, and tomorrow you can do something about it. But the main attention should be ongoing over your day with a Friend who gave the day to you and lived it through with you. Your day then becomes not a disconnected series of events you have endured, but a whole, something you have summed up and possessed.

Prayer of Good Fortune

Another kind of prayer that is sometimes even fun is to ponder the endless numbers of lucky chances that have enriched your life. (Chance, or design?) I think sometimes: What if my parents had never met? What if my dad, who was a truck driver, had not stopped into the store where Mom worked? What if he'd been too shy to ask for a date? What if they'd said, "One child is enough"?

119

My mother had three or four miscarriages before she had me; why not me, too? Children are born deaf or blind, physically impaired, unwanted, battered; why not me? At one time the people I love most were total strangers; what happened that they have become so precious, so essential to my happiness?

Of course there are no answers to those questions. And one can say, "Well, if such-and-such had never happened, I'd be none the wiser." But the fact is such-and-such *did* happen, and the joy they have given me is something I did nothing to deserve. I have to be grateful to Someone! And gratitude is prayer indeed.

EXERCISE

Begin with relaxation, deep-breathing exercises. Feel the breath arise from your lower abdomen and up through your lungs and out through your nose. Keep a steady, calming pace.

Step 1. Think back to the luckiest event of your life. Was it the day you were born? Was it the day you were baptized? Imagine the event and the happiness associated with it. Be grateful for such good fortune.

Step 2. Think back to the worst event of your life. Imagine the sadness associated with this event. Ponder how the happy day and the sad day are really related. Reflect on how God's design is in both the good and the not-so-good moments.

TRANSFORMATIVE PRAYERS

If our eyes and ears are sensitized enough, God speaks to us in all kinds of ways, not merely through the Scriptures and through nature. God speaks to us, calls to us, in the eyes of the needy (and not just the materially needy), in the eyes of giggling children, in the averted eyes of people who think they want to be anonymous and safe from either pain or love.

In the same way, we have all kinds of ways of talking back to God, lying all over the place, if we have the sensitivity to notice them and the imagination to turn them into prayers. Anyone who has seen the serigraph posters of Corita Kent knows even advertising jingles can be turned into visual prayers.

It takes a little tinkering but, with the right understanding, some of the billboard slogans along the highway can turn into secret messages between you and God, like "You only go around once in life, so grab for all the gusto you can get." That says, as Jesus did, "I have come to cast fire on the earth," or "I have come that they may have life, and have it more abundantly."

✻ Prayer-Songs

Not many realize that the Newley-Bricusse song "Who Can I Turn To?" was not written to be sung by a man to a woman or a woman to a man. It was written as a prayer addressed to God.

There are other obvious songs one can turn into prayers without any difficulty at all: "I Don't Know How to Love Him" from *Jesus Christ Superstar,* many of the Simon and Garfunkel and Beatles oldies, especially George Harrison's "My Sweet Lord."

But there are other songs that merely have to have the "You" capitalized to be turned into prayers. For old-timers like me, Ira Gershwin and Cole Porter are treasure houses: "I'll be seeing You, in all the old familiar places...." and "You are the promised touch of springtime, that makes the lonely winter seem long," and "You're the top!" These were all written originally as songs for two lovers. But what else is praying but a song sung by two lovers?

EXERCISE

Begin with deep-breathing exercises. Then pause for a moment and let your mind ramble over the lyrics of your favorite secular songs. Five'll getcha ten you can think of one that can be turned into a prayer before a minute is up.

Newspaper-Prayer

Even the daily paper can open a way to hear God
speaking, and it can provide matter for all kinds of
conversations with God. Just as Yahweh spoke to Is-
rael through the plagues of Egypt and invasions by
foreign conquerors, God still speaks to us through
the events of this week's history.

Every picture of urban blight or ecological cor-
ruption says the same thing God said to Adam and
Eve when they gave them dominion over the earth.
Every picture from the horn of Africa or Eastern Europe is another call to "beat your swords into plow-
shares" or you will have more of this. Every two-
page supermarket spread says, "I was hungry…I was
naked…did you even notice?"

I must give a very strong caution here, however.
Someone who becomes aware of world-wide human suffering is in danger of "the liberal guilt complex." Schools, with the very best of intentions, very
unwisely generate this unfocused, low-grade guilt
which can stir up a nameless frustration within us
and thereby spoil whatever effectiveness we might
have had. "What are you doing about the poor
starving babies in Somalia? The refugees? The wars
and famine and ecology and crime and mental ill-
ness and the birthrate and obscenity and…."

"*STOP!* I have only two hands and one heart! I have
only a twenty-four-hour day and a seventy-year life!
I can be in only one place at a time! *I can't* take care
of all those things." And so we give up.

Such people should be assured they can't expect themselves to be responsible for everything, but they should also be reminded they are responsible for what they *can* do.

124

If we narrow our attentions to one or two needy areas, we'll be doing just fine. One way even kids can lessen human suffering just a bit: once every month or so, send the price of one movie ticket to a fund for needy children. Another idea: go through your closet and drawers and give away everything you haven't worn in a year. Obviously, you don't need it; someone else does.

The purpose of letting the newspaper reveal God to us is that it scales down our own small troubles closer to the proportions they have in God's eyes, sensitizes us to those in need who *are* within reach.

EXERCISE

As usual, begin with preliminary deep breathing. Pick up a copy of the daily newspaper or a weekly news magazine. Try reading the paper or magazine the way you would guess Jesus would read it. Try to feel the way he would feel, and then pray the way he would pray.

He was a realist, remember. He did not try to take over the centers of power and communication in Rome. He lived in a little backwater of a place and physically touched few people. Yet what he began has changed the world, and it has lasted for twenty centuries. That is worth praying over.

Prayers That Were Never
Meant to Be Prayers

The idea for such prayers came to me through Betsy Caprio's fine book *Experiments in Prayer.* Her book consists of ways to find prayers in the least likely places—novels, poems, plays, ads, or the visual prayers of Corita Kent. The one I like best is one that apparently flashed out at her from the dull pages of a French grammar and which she turned into an unexpected little speech to God: "I love You, I have loved You, I will love You."

The poems of e.e. cummings are a bit elusive at times. But the very thorniness makes some of his poems a kind of koan, which can be mulled and distilled and made to seep into the spirit. Here is an example.

no time ago
or else a life
walking in the dark
i met christ

jesus)my heart
flopped over
and lay still
while he passed (as

close as i'm to you
yes closer
made of nothing
except loneliness

Another is my favorite cummings poem:

*i thank You God for most this amazing
day:for the leaping greenly spirits of trees
and a blue true dream of sky; and for
    everything
which is natural which is infinite
    which is yes*

*(i who have died am alive again today,
and this is the sun's birthday; this is the birth
day of life and of love and wings: and
    of the gay
great happening illimitably earth)*

*how should tasting touching hearing seeing
breathing any—lifted from the no
of all nothing—human merely being
doubt unimaginable You?*

*(now the ears of my ears awake and
now the eyes of my eyes are opened)*

Those last two lines are about as good a description of meditative prayer as I have ever read. It is a realization which a very good actor once shared with me about plays: "God is the only one who creates anything; we—even artists—do not create; we merely discover."

Everyone should find his or her own not-meant-to-be-prayers. Here are a few I have found:

I was trying to make
my mouth say I would do
the right thing...
but deep down in me
I knowed it was a lie,
and He knowed it.
You can't pray a lie—
I found that out.

Mark Twain

Everyone in the world is Christ and
they are all crucified.

Sherwood Anderson

i have noticed that when chickens quit quarrel-
ing over their food they often find that there is
enough for all of them i wonder if it might not be
the same with the human race

Don Marquis

Among animals, one has a sense of humor.

Marianne Moore

When custom presses on the souls apart
Who seek a God not worshipped by the herd
Forth, to the wilderness the chosen start
Content with ruin, having but the Word.

John Masefield

There is no indispensable man.

Franklin Roosevelt

For man, the vast marvel
is to be alive.
...we ought to dance with rapture
that we should be alive and in the flesh,
and part of the living incarnate
cosmos. I am part of the sun as my
eye is part of me.
That I am part of the earth my
feet know perfectly, and my blood
is part of the sea.
My soul knows that I am part of the
human race, my soul is an organic
part of the great human race,
as my spirit is part of my nation.

D. H. Lawrence

*Our lives are merely strange
dark interludes in the
electrical display of
God the Father!*

Eugene O'Neill

❦

God is a verb, not a noun.

Buckminster Fuller

*The Future is something which
everyone reaches at the rate
of sixty minutes an hour,
whatever he does,
whoever he is.*

C. S. Lewis

*If you forgive people enough you
belong to them, and they to you,
whether either person likes it or not.
Squatters' rights of the heart.*

James Hilton

*It is often easier to fight for
principles than to live up to them.*

Adlai Stevenson

EXERCISE

Begin with the deep-breathing, relaxation routine. Make contact with your inner being, finding solace and solitude.

Select a book of poems or quotations. Place the volume in your lap, and let your mind's eye roam through the book's contents, and select a passage or part of a poem that is of significance to you.

Ponder on the meaning of the saying, relating it to a prayerful context.

Work-Prayer

Even Our Lady didn't spend the entire day with all her thoughts on Jesus; there certainly must have been almost endless chores to do. Teresa of Avila, a real heavyweight in praying, had to haul herself out of her cell and sit for hours listening with her whole attention to the problems of her nuns. Thomas Merton, the Trappist monk, had to limit his time of actual meditation because he was expected not only to write books but also to take a hand at washing the dishes and hoeing the fields.

Even those whose prayer-lives are light years ahead of our own have to take their direct awareness away from God and turn it back on the world God gave us to enliven.

But our work, too, can be sharing aliveness with God. The daily round of housework, office work, school work, manual work is a contact with the surfaces under which the life-giving presence of God waits to be noticed and brought closer to the surface. But how?

The first step is the realization that God truly *is* in all things, even in unpleasant things such as memorizing French irregular verbs, or cleaning up after the dog, or typing lists, or sweeping streets. At times, though, it seems like playing hide-and-seek when the other Player has up and gone home.

At times like that, you must begin by trying to find some inner value in the job itself. *Why* am I forced to memorize these verbs when I'll probably never go to France? If the only reason you can come up with is, "Oh, well, because 'they' told me I have to," or "Everybody has to," then you're not there yet. *Why* do "they" tell you to, and *why* does everybody have to?

The same is true of moving the same dust from the same furniture week after week, of hammering nails, operating a computer. If the only reason is that someone will gripe if you don't do it, if it's only for the paycheck, you're still not there yet. Nor is "God has set me to this" good enough. If the only reason for doing the job comes from outside the job, then there will be little more aliveness or joy or even simple satisfaction in your work than a horse finds pulling a cart or a fax machine takes in spitting out messages.

Only you know what jobs you have that seem purposeless. So don't sit there and expect me to hammer them out for you. Go sit down with God awhile and listen. Don't talk. Listen.

Hint: often the tedious jobs are essential for something else we want and truly love.

Once you find the inner value of the jobs you can't escape, a purpose that satisfies not the surface of your mind but the depths of your heart, you will almost automatically find a newer, richer *quality* in your work. The person who sees not just a paycheck but people's lives improved by his or her work will not go at it like a mindless zombie. A homemaker who gets inside the breadwinner's shoes at the moment of returning home from work, who understands, will not be content with preparing a nonnourishing dinner. And if the breadwinner does the same, gets inside the homemaker's day, the breadwinner will not gripe about TV dinners when that's the best that can be done that day.

Kahlil Gibran wrote, "Work is love made visible." And if it's not, the job either shouldn't be done or should be reassessed. If your job is to clean public restrooms, clean those rooms as if the people you love best were going to use them. After all, if I understand Jesus rightly, no matter who uses them will be your brothers and sisters.

Once you go at the dishes or the attic or the weekend essay the way you suspect Jesus would have done them, you will begin to see that Presence emerging even from the most unpromising places, even from the most boring tasks, because in order to draw that aliveness to the surface, some of your own aliveness has to go in from this side.

Our Father is helplessly in love with aliveness. God cannot resist coming forward to meet it, especially when it is aliveness expended in apparently unpromising places or with unpromising people.

Consider what God was able to do with the grumbling Hebrew slaves of Egypt. Consider what God was able to do with a backwoods rabbi, crucified as a criminal. Consider what God was able to do with a ragtag handful of cowards, once they had opened themselves to the aliveness of Pentecost. God won't be outdone in sharing aliveness.

This transformation of work into prayer has to come first from seeing a reason within the work itself, not by pouring the Morning Offering over it like baptismal water and then grumbling your way through it like a slave. But once you see the inner value any work has (or else it isn't worth doing), no matter how tedious, then it does help to snatch a moment to realize that you are not alone doing it, that there is another Person (in fact three of them!) at your side, attentive and caring.

EXERCISE

Begin, as usual with a deep breath and a moment of consecration. It is good to begin the first job of the morning with a moment of re-collection of self and of the Aliveness within you. Then again after your coffee break, and again after lunch. But this shouldn't become the half-hearted, no-minded formality most of us associate with the quick grace before meals or the droning mind-in-neutral prayers before class in school. Those are so often times when the words are said by someone else, while I spend time wondering whether there are enough pieces of chicken or whether the teacher will call on me today.

The prayer at the beginning of a segment of work should not merely be a "prayer," as a child would understand praying. It should try to focus into conscious awareness the Presence who will do the day's work with you. It's only a moment, but if it's important and prayer has begun to seam your life together, you'll remember to do it at each new phase of the day.

Then once the "connection" has been made, you will forget God no doubt, just as a boy could stare with utter intensity at the girl across the aisle while the teacher is handing out the final exam. But once the exam's begun, she could be Godzilla for all he knows. As Teresa of Avila said when accused of enjoying eating partridge with too obvious relish: "When it's time for prayer, pray; when it's time for partridge, partridge!"

These are only a few ways in which you can transform the objects and events and persons of every day into a sharing of aliveness with God. Like every artist, God is lurking inside everything they have made, waiting to be noticed. Everything speaks of God, if "the eyes of my ears awake...the eyes of my eyes are opened."

135

PRAYING TOGETHER

Most of us are shy. In fact, I'd be willing to bet that, under even the most brassy and cocksure exteriors, we are all basically wary. It takes at least a bit of gumption to say to somebody we don't know very well, "Hey, howdja like to go to a movie?" We all can imagine, then, the inner fears triggered by "Hey, howdja like to pray together?"

Praying together is something we'd all more or less rather leave to the packed anonymity of Sunday Mass. Which is precisely why so many find Sunday Mass boring. It is packed and anonymous, uptight and not personally involving. If you could ever find a congregation—however small—that would let down the defenses and really release its inner power in unashamed prayer, the Church finally would be in danger of setting the earth on fire, as it was told to do.

No one would leave that community saying, "The Church really ought to...." They would say instead, "We ought to...," since they would realize not just in their minds but in the depths of themselves that we *are* the Church.

Sunday Masses should be a sharing of prayer. Let's face it: in 99 percent of the cases, it isn't. It may well be a few hundred people who gather and pray silently within themselves, one-on-one with God, who also obediently, if halfheartedly, interrupt their "real praying" to moo back the responses to the priest.

But Sunday Mass really is the priest's show, right? Recently he's been given a few co-stars (as in the early Greek theater; there's still hope) to read a bit and tell people when to stand and sit (which they already know). But in general all the action really takes place "up there," no? Sadly, that's not the way the first Mass was, nor is it how all repetitions were intended to be.

It would be exciting if each member of the congregation got involved! But that's not likely. I remember in college when we were trying to get a friend of ours to cut a class one Friday and hitch to a basketball game in Boston. He said, "Weeeeelll. If you can get six or eight other guys to do it, I'll think about it." From that moment on, his name was "Guts."

The same thing is true of making Mass come alive. If everyone else dares to throw off their uptightness— the way people do at a rock concerts or when cheering at a championship game—I'm willing to let down my defenses, too; then I'll have the guts. Instead we cringe when Dad sings so loud, and Mom utters prayer so audibly, and the kids fidget. Of course they fidget. They're bored silly. Mass—as it's ordinarily executed—is a strong incentive to disbelief. And if we were more honest than brainwashed, we'd admit it. Then we might set about doing something to change it.

But it is easier to stand in back. After all, nobody else is dropping their guards, right? Why should I? Personally, I lay a great deal of blame for this on the priest leading the congregation. If he's as formal as a visiting diplomat, it's little wonder men and women who have shared the same bed for twenty years will turn to one another at the greeting of peace and *shake hands!* If the celebrant is overly folksy and cute, it's little wonder the parents think the Mass is "for the kids." If he performs his chores with all the exuberance of a conductor calling out station stops, the Mass becomes a testimony to faith only in the same way as enduring the iron maiden was.

139

But in places where Mass is a bore, the blame is not *all* on the celebrant. You could have a celebrant with all the pizzazz of a Las Vegas entertainer, accompanied by the Mormon Tabernacle Choir, but if the congregation is locked in family cocoons (and each member further cocooned within that one), passive and biddable as sheep, the Mass has no chance of enlivening anyone.

Because of this reluctance we all seem to share, it may seem difficult to entertain the possibility of sharing prayer in a small group. However, it really is nowhere near as intimidating as it sounds.

Many who "teach" methods of prayer often begin with this kind of shared prayer, reading a passage of Scripture, pausing for personal reflections, and then—if anyone wishes—he or she may express a prayer out loud. In my opinion, it might be better to allow participants to get a bit more used to personal meditative prayer before adding the intimidation of doing it with others. Once one has mastered a bit the processes of relaxing, focusing, remaining in silence without uneasiness, then I believe shared prayer will be less daunting.

As with Mass, there are several practical advantages of praying together. For one thing, it keeps you at it, even at times when you were just about ready to throw it away as a bad job—which is precisely the time when those who doggedly persist break through! As with having an advisor, praying in a small group with others is also reassurance that you are not alone in believing, in praying, in trying to continue to grow in prayer.

But over and above the practical advantages, shared prayer can be a very enriching experience. Every time I have done it, I've come away enlivened by the honesty and self-forgetfulness of the people with whom I've prayed. It takes any of us a bit of self-exposure to speak aloud about things we have formerly shared only with God. But overcoming that fear can itself give you a jubilant feeling.

Of course, if one is frightened, then he or she has not really heard the message of the gospels, which says we should not be afraid. Jesus' first word upon entering a room was, "Peace!" He said also that those who trust him and his Spirit would be able to handle serpents and cast out devils. Next to that, praying aloud together looks relatively easier.

On the one hand, such prayer sessions should not be the occasion for dredging up one's deepest problems; they take too much explanation, and these meetings are for prayer, not for psychiatric examination. Prayer is not group therapy, and if anyone "takes over," the leader should have the courage to step in and remonstrate (gently) with him or her. If not, forget it.

On the other hand, prayer sessions together should not be mere off-the-top-of-the-head prayers for the poor and unwanted, like many of the generic prayers at the offertory of Mass. Shared prayer is not "general prayer"; it is personal prayer, together. What one says should echo up from the depths of the self. Just as in personal private prayer one wants to contact his or her genuine and undisguised self, so too does one want to do this in personal shared prayer as well. One can be truly personal and genuine in this somewhat public prayer without baring his or her inmost secrets or hiding behind airy generalities. Moreover, the Scripture passage or reading gives a kind of center around which the prayers will often satellize.

How to Share Prayer

The first thing to find is a suitable room. If at all possible, it should not be too big. (Nor should the group.) It is good, too, if the room is as far away as possible from the loudest distractions and able to be darkened if the group wants it that way.

If the participants have some experience of private meditation, they should be a bit more adept than others at shutting out distracting noises—passing airplanes, voices down the hall, telephones. After a while, such distractions can be no more audible than a voice telling you to take out the garbage when you are engrossed in music. Still, it is best to avoid noise as much as possible.

Make sure there's a sign on the door telling potential intruders to get lost. And if there's a phone in the room, unplug it.

If the room has a rug, so much the better. If individuals want them and they are storable, pillows and chairs help people assume whatever positions they find most conducive to peace and concentration. If there are no pillows, people can bundle their jackets and use them. Take off your shoes and your watches. If you have to limit the time, put an alarm clock in a drawer where you can't hear it ticking.

Sometimes it helps to sit in a circle with a lighted candle in the center. The candle helps concentration, and it keeps the more wary from wondering if "they're all looking at me." But if someone finds it better to sit facing the wall, so be it.

Format for Shared Prayer

As in all times of meditative prayer, take a few moments to do relaxing exercises—especially here where potential distractions multiply and uptightness may make some members focus on their own uneasiness rather than on their deepest selves. Shared prayer is a more complex way to pray: not only focused on oneself but also reaching out to the other selves.

Then let someone read a very short passage from Scripture or a poem, or play some evocative music. Use any of the methods suggested in these pages, and there are thousands more.

143

The next stage is silent reflection: just sit, ponder, reflect, pray. Suggest beforehand that no one ought to "burst into words" too soon. Then, if the Spirit moves anyone, let him or her express a short prayer out loud—not to the group but to the Presence on whom the group is focused. Again, beforehand, suggest subtly that this isn't a time to prove one's piety—or one's verbal facility—but one's humility.

People should speak when—and if—they choose. Never go in order around the circle, so that someone has to fret that "I'm on deck, and I better come up with something impressive." The Spirit designates who's next.

Avoiding Some Difficulties With Shared Prayer

There are the same dangers to shared prayer as there are with so-called "dialogue homilies." Sometimes there will be a member who feels compelled to give "subtle sermons" or tell the group "what we all ought to do." Not only are these ordinarily tedious and at times unconsciously condescending, but they tend to focus the attention of the group on the speaker instead of on the Listener. If it occurs, someone should speak to the individual outside the session and privately. Just tell the person long prayers make the others fidgety. If the person is sincere, he or she will take the hint. If not, as Benedict says, "Let two stout monks attempt to reason with him."

Let the members understand that no one *has* to say anything. If someone says nothing, don't worry about him or her or that the silence has to go on and on until each person has spoken. An individual may be too shy, or too deeply touched, or too involved with the Presence. The Spirit will move each one in a unique way. Otherwise, it becomes a roll-call—which is precisely what all of you came together to forget in the first place.

Also, don't fear long pauses. For some reason, we fear empty air, as if it were the same thing as "dead air" to a radio station engineer. It's not dead at all but very much alive. Nor should anyone fear "I've used up my turn and shouldn't speak again." Unlike lightning, the Spirit can strike as often as she chooses in the same place.

The last thing one should fear is "what they'll think of me, or of what I'm saying, or the way I'm saying it." Check the egos at the door. As the gospel says, the Spirit will tell you what to say and how to say it.

Jesus said it all in four words: "Do not be afraid."

And let the last word be his, too: "Peace."

WILLIAM J. O'MALLEY, S.J.,

is the author of twenty-three books and nearly one hundred articles. Earlier works include *Why Be Catholic?* (Crossroad); *Building Your Own Conscience (Batteries Not Included)* (Tabor); and *Yielding: Prayers for Those in Need of Hope* (Liguori Publications). Father O'Malley teaches and resides in the Bronx, New York.